Alexander Hogg

The Railroad as an Element in Education

Alexander Hogg

The Railroad as an Element in Education

ISBN/EAN: 9783337236205

Printed in Europe, USA, Canada, Australia, Japan

Cover: Foto ©Suzi / pixelio.de

More available books at **www.hansebooks.com**

AS AN

LEMENT IN EDUCATION,

AN ADDRESS

BEFORE THE INTERNATIONAL CONGRESS OF EDUCATORS,

WORLD'S EXPOSITION,

NEW ORLEANS.

BY

PROF. ALEX. HOGG, M. A.

SUP'T PUBLIC SCHOOLS, FORT WORTH.

EDITION OF 1888, WITH ADDENDA.

LOUISVILLE:
PRINTED FOR THE AUTHOR.
1889.

DEDICATED TO SCIENCE AND SKILL

BY THE AUTHOR.

GEORGE STEPHENSON.

THE RAILROAD

AS AN

ELEMENT IN EDUCATION.

Mr. President:

Steam is well-born; is a lineal descendant of the four elements of the ancients—earth, air, fire, and water — has survived, lived through more than two thousand years, gaining strength from its own usefulness and age; is to-day in the full vigor of manhood. As a motive power steam was known 130 years B. C.* Hero of Egypt exhibited his Eolipile, an apparatus with a metallic boiler, provided at the top with two horizontal jet-pipes bent into the form of an **S**. The steam, escaping from these jets and reacting upon the air, gave a rotary motion to the pipes. Barker's centrifugal mill is an example of this kind of action.

Blanco de Goray, of Barcelona, as far back as 1543, propelled with steam a vessel of two hundred tons.

But passing over historical details—leaving out the controversies of aspiring inventors and discoverers—I come to a year in our civilization memorable for rich results.

*Spiritalia seu Pneumatica.

(3)

In 1776, the "transmutations" of alchemy, the *ideal* of Paracelsus, gave birth to the *real* of Priestley and Lavoisier, and chemistry as a practical science is announced to the world. This same year Adam Smith published his Wealth of Nations. This same year the Declaration of Independence was proclaimed by the Continental Congress. This same year Watt produced—perfected his "improved," his "successful" steam-engine.

The man of science can, with pardonable pride, exclaim, "Arithmetic fails to enumerate the 'agents' and 'reagents' of chemistry!" The political philosopher can point to the real wealth of the nations as the best result of his science ; the statesman can, with true patriotism, refer to our peaceful, our happy republic as the legitimate result of the Declaration.

Individuals may boast of the triumphs of these, but the millions whose burthens have been lightened and lifted, who are fed and clothed by the diversified labors of steam, may be excused too — will be pardoned—for their appreciation of the result which gave to the world the steam-engine of James Watt.

Patriotic as I am, and claiming as I do for our Fulton the first successful application of steam to navigation, in the Clermont (1807), I as cheerfully accord to the mother-country the honor due George Stephenson (1829), for his successful "run" in the Rocket over the Rainhill trial course.

It is a remarkable fact that within the last one hundred years science has made its most rapid strides.   Steam and electricity, motor and messenger, have vied with, not rivaled, each other in *transporting* and *transmitting*, until "*there is no speech nor language where their voice is not heard.   Their line is gone out through all the earth, and their words to the end of the world.*"

Classical scholars have insisted that our word "educate" is from *educere* —to draw out ; and hence they have taught that education is a "pumping" process, that it is all in and within the mind of the child, the learner, and must be drawn out ; and thus to their theory is due largely the one-sided instruction, or the total disregard of every other method.   The truth is, our word "educate" is from a different word—it is from *educare*, which means "to bring up," "to train," "to develop," "to increase and give power to."   There can be no mistake from this view, that there is a pouring-into as well as a pumping-out in the process of education.

HARTFORD

NEW YORK

Y

PAPER.

BOSTON

X

TIN FOIL.

COFFEY SC.

"Each of the pens is simply a small-pointed iron needle. Now suppose that both of the pens are moved at the same time and with the same rapidity across their respective sheets. Then the electric current, decomposing the prussiate of potash, will cause the needle in New York to trace a continuous blue line on Y, until the needle in Boston reaches a line of sealing-wax on X, when the circuit is broken as it passes over this line. At the same time there is a break in the continuity of the line traced on Y. If, further, each needle is moved down a hair's breadth each time, it traverses its respective sheet, then we shall have an exact fac-simile of the writing on the tin-foil produced on the chemically-prepared paper. Pen-and-ink sketches of photographs and other pictures may be transmitted in the same way."

I have no war against the classics. So far from it, I assert to-day that there can be no "liberal education" without the classics.

Among these, however, I claim the first place in order and importance shall be assigned to our mother tongue. The Greek knew no other than his own language, nor did the Roman go abroad to study until he had mastered the Latin. Why, then, should we ignore, why should we be so slow to acknowledge, the claims of modern science?

In the demands made by the progressive development of railroad construction, and the improvement in that vast field alone, every science and every department of science is laid under contribution, until we have here the fullest and happiest illustration of the great law of "supply and demand."

A motive power greater than that of man or horse, an improved steam-engine, is called for, and James Watt presents his. And now a locomotive is needed that shall transfer this mighty energy, adapt it to the road, and George Stephenson controls with his own hand the throttle of his own engine. And now a trestle, and now a bridge, and now a suspension bridge, and that, too, across Niagara, and the occasion—science, conscious of this new requisition—gives to the world John A. Roebling.

Harmonizing circumstances—Time, the great arbiter, comes in, and so orders it that Robert, the son of George Stephenson, should pass over Niagara River in a railway train, and on the suspension bridge which he had but lately declared to be an impracticable undertaking.

The purpose of this great engineer's visit to this country was to make an inspection of the location for the celebrated tubular bridge at Montreal. Stephenson had criticised and condemned the suspension principle, and had approved the tubular girder for railway traffic.

At that time doctors of science—engineers—differed as to their theories, but, as now, they also agreed upon the facts as exhibited in the results.

In 1874 I visited Niagara Falls, spent two days, was delighted, amazed, and awed in turn at this wonderful manifestation, this remarkable phenomenon of nature.

From the Falls I went to the suspension bridge. Upon this structure stood two through express trains awaiting the signals to move on their ways, east and west. At the appointed moment they did move. Without tremor or oscillation that bridge sustained its accustomed load, performed its duty, as it had done thousands of times before, as it had done fifty times that very day.

When I saw this bridge spanning this angry river, supporting these heavily laden trains, I felt this inspiration; I said, "This bridge for the *creature* is equal to yon cataract for the CREATOR."

But again, another demand—a higher principle still—a fiat had gone forth that not only shall "*Every valley be exalted, but every mountain and hill shall be made low; and the crooked shall be made straight, and the rough places plain.*"

Streams, rivulets, rivers had been bridged, the valley had been exalted; the crooked route must now be made straight, the mountain must be made low. No longer can time be consumed in searching out the passable passes, in following the tortuous gorge. The yawning chasm, the deep cañon, the treacherous glacier, the awful avalanche, snow and ice, mountain-pass and mountain-peak—all, all must be shunned—must be left to enjoy undisturbed their lofty abode amid its chilly, frozen environments.

Whether Pyrenees or Alps, Alleghany or Hoosac, all ranges standing in the way of the locomotive must be made low, must be TUNNELED. Science, quietly observing what is going on, anticipating these new and still greater demands, accordingly prepares for yet greater results, and at this juncture and for this stupendous work furnishes both the engineering skill to conduct and the new motors, Burleigh drills, and air-compressors to perform the boring, and dynamite to do the blasting, and we have Mount Cenis Tunnel, a trifle less than *eight miles* in length, thirteen and a half years building, at a cost of $15,000,000; St. Gothard, *nine and a quarter miles*, seven and a half years building, at a cost of $9,700,000, consuming half the time, at two thirds the cost of the Cenis Tunnel; the Hoosac Tunnel, some five miles in length, eleven years in building, costing $13,000,000.

One among the first railroad tunnels in the United States was the Alleghany Portage double-track, nine hundred feet long, costing some $21,840.

I must be pardoned for mentioning, in this connection, that here particularly the skill of the engineer is tested in the use of the most accurate

instruments and of the most celebrated makers. In boring the Mosconetcon
Tunnel on the Lehigh Valley Railroad—a work less in extent than some,
but said to be of as great magnitude, on account of the presence of water
and other difficulties, as any of the American tunnels—the east and west
headings met in December, 1874, whereupon it was found that the error in
level and *alignment* was less than half an inch.

THE BROOKLYN BRIDGE.

To be an engineer in the full and complete sense of the term embraces
all sciences, pure and applied. Nor are the languages to be left out.
Through the Latin we learn of Cæsar's bridge, through the Greek of
Xerxes' bridge of boats (*pontoons*). That is not a complete curriculum that
would leave French and German out of the engineer's course. Our Latin
teachers are very proud when their brightest scholars can translate the
description of Cæsar's bridge. It is considered hard Latin; it is given as

a task—not for the information about the bridge, but because of the difficulty of the translation.

Now, Mr. President, turn your countenance upward; exercise the prerogative you enjoy above the rest of the animals (" . . . *quae natura prona*"), behold the arches that support this Grand Structure! Tell me if there is not more study, more beauty in one of these than in a whole book of Cæsar?

In 1883, and in this country, there has been completed and opened the greatest structure—the grandest monument to skill and science—to father and son, to John A. and Washington A. Roebling—to the former for the conception, to the latter for the construction of the Brooklyn Bridge—the longest span in the world. In the building of this highway, virtually making New York and Brooklyn one city, the entire domain of science has been laid under contribution. Every formula of mathematics, every discovery of chemistry, every law of physics, all have furnished their quota. Every department of human industry, every tool invented by the ingenuity of man has borne its part in the final result. Without the most recent discoveries of science, the converting of iron into steel by the pneumatic process, the bridge in its present form could not have been built.

I can not describe in detail all the creative and constructive efforts of the human mind in this great work. It is not necessary; it is finished—"*Finis coronat opus.*"

All this, however, is upon but one side, the department of construction, the building of railroads.

There is still another side, the operating department, in which to accuracy of calculation must be added discretion, sound judgment, and all the higher qualities of head, and heart too. Here we learn—we take an account of exceedingly small things; here we hear the name of the nonentity, the imaginary *mill*, and use it in actual daily transactions:

"So many tons a mile at so many mills per ton."

"It will cost so many mills to move such freight; therefore, in order to pay dividends and cover operating expenses, we must charge so much per hundred."

The tables—operating expenses—have these items: "The amount of coal used this year compared with last on Division —— was 1.8 pounds more, or 2.3 pounds less per mile."

In what school can a pupil be found who would distribute the tax-assessment for eleven hundred miles of railway passing through twenty-nine counties, and the miles and *hundredths* of a mile in each county to be taken into account, each county assessing a different valuation, and balance up the whole to within *five mills*, one half of one cent?

These are some of the problems, and these are some of the questions that are solved by the railroad accountants.

The curse of our schools, and colleges, and universities too, is the want of accuracy. And I am not sure but the careless use of slates and black-boards has much to do with it. It is so easy to say, "Oh! that is wrong—rub it out." In railroading you can not "rub it out."*

The dispatcher who sits at his table with fifty—a hundred and fifty—trains on the rail has more responsibility every way than the general who directs an army.

"*Some one had blundered,*"

was said when, at Balaklava,

"Then they rode back, but not—
Not the six hundred."

Some one has blundered in Egypt. Had Palmerston built a railroad from Cairo to Khartoum, there would not now be a rebel in the Soudan to annoy Gladstone.

Your World's Exposition reminds me of the Centennial (1876) at Phil-adelphia. The latter was full of examples—fruitful illustrations of what the accuracy and precision in railroad managements accomplish in safety to property and person.

The Pennsylvania road alone gave receipts for 16,039 cars of building material—for 4,116 cars of exhibits placed within the Centennial grounds, without a single claim being made for damage. The total number of pieces of baggage received and delivered at the several stations amounted to

*You do not find slates and blackboards in the rooms of accountants.

730,486 pieces. Of these, *twenty-six* pieces were lost, the claims for which amounted to $1,906.99.

Total number of passengers from May 10th to November 10th, 4,955,-712, carried without injury to a single one.

Add to this that during the year 1876 this road moved 17,064,953 tons of freight and 18,363,366 passengers without loss of life or harm to any one.

With these facts before me I am ready to believe the following: "A French statistician observes that if a person were to live continually in a railway carriage, and spend all his time in railway traveling, the chances of his dying from a railway accident would not occur until he was *nine hundred* years old."

But the railroad is solving other problems—social problems, commercial problems, farming problems.

The poet has said:

"Seas shall join the regions they divide;"

The railroad answers: And continents shall unite the oceans they separate. The rich valleys of the interior, the fertile plains of the "Far West," are made neighbors to,—find markets upon the very shores of the Atlantic, all by and through the agency of the railroad.

We hear a great deal about the Great West! Pray, what has made the West so great?

Not greatness of territory solely—not great distances, but the potentiality, the living, working capacity of the locomotive—the greatest pioneer, the greatest missionary ever sent out by Church or State.

What makes Chicago the successful rival of New York? The latter is the senior of the former, not only by *scores*, but by *two hundred* years.

The ten thousand miles of railway tributary to Chicago—the seven hundred trains (three hundred and fifty arriving and three hundred and fifty departing daily), with their heavily laden cars of both passengers and freight—have something to do with the prosperity, the metropolitan pretentions of the "Lake City."

What will make your city the rival of both New York and Chicago?

Not because she is the outlet of the Mississippi Basin, but because she is the eastern terminus of the railroads of the Pacific Slope, the Southwest, the Northwest.

The superintendent of our last—the tenth—census says: "The closeness with which the center of population, through such rapid westward movement as has been recorded, has clung to the parallel of 39° of latitude can not fail to be noticed."

He does not, however, say a word as to the cause of this singular movement westward four hundred and fifty-seven miles in ninety years. Near and upon the 38°, 39°, and 40° of latitude may be found three of the great trunk railways.

But their location is still another problem. The peculiar climate, productiveness of the soil, and the early settlement of this region have all something to do with it. Here is problem growing out of problem, fruitful each to the student of social philosophy.

But again. I argue more directly, because more demonstratively tangible, that the school interest, the schools themselves, have flourished and spread their influence in the direct ratio of the number of miles of railroad in the State. Massachusetts, at home and abroad, stands at the head of our school system; nor is it disputed that in her borders we find models of true culture and refinement. Massachusetts has a mile of railroad to every four square miles of territory.

This is a case from the extreme East. I take an example from what used to be termed the West, now about the middle of our country: Ohio has a mile of railroad for every six square miles of territory. Ohio has pretty good school facilities, and of late has furnished her full quota of presidents.

But select at will any State, and upon the map mark the seats of institutions of learning—schools, academies, colleges, and universities—and you will find them all arranged along the lines of the great railroads.

England and Wales, Belgium, Switzerland, and Scotland possess the greatest railway facilities. These also enjoy the greatest freedom, the best systems of schools of all the European States.

But to come still nearer: Texas is an example in which from being the largest State in the Union territorially, she has become also greater in resources than any of her sister States of the South, simply on account of the indissoluble bond between her school-lands and her railroads.

Of seventy-four cities and towns assuming control of their schools, supplementing the amount received from the State (five dollars for each pupil of scholastic age annually) by a special tax, sixty-six of these are directly upon the lines of railways, while the remaining eight are of easy access to railroads.

We hear a great deal about what "The Fathers of Texas" have done for the education of all the children of the State; the thousands of leagues of land reserved for the counties — the millions of acres for the general school fund.

These historians should go a little further, and tell us what these "millions of acres" were worth before the railroad companies surveyed and brought these lands to the attention of the world.

It is true that the railroads received sixteen sections of land for every mile of road built, conditioned, however, upon the companies surveying their own, together with an equal number of sections (*alternates*) for the schools.

The entire expense of surveying and returning a double set of field notes to the General Land Office, at Austin, was borne by the respective railroads.

These lands were, for the most part, hundreds of miles beyond civilization; indeed, the roads have been extended more rapidly than a paying traffic would warrant in order to develop their lands, to bring them into market.

The Texas & Pacific wore out its main line of 444 miles in building the extension west of 616 miles—was a practical example of the problem: "How far would a boy travel, starting from a basket two yards from the first egg, and carrying singly to the basket one hundred eggs, two yards apart, in a straight line?" *

But whatever develops, enhances the railroad "sections," enhances the school "alternates," until lands heretofore not commanding twenty-five

---

* Some idea can be formed of the amount of *wear* and *tear* on the road, when it is understood that the boy traveled 11 miles 840 yards.

cents an acre are now readily sold for two dollars; or, the railroads have increased the school funds *eight-fold*, have multiplied their values until **Texas** boasts of a free-school fund of *ninety-five million dollars*—a fund that will yield, at five per cent per annum, $4,750,000. In valuation, the report of the Comptroller shows the railroads to be the third in order. Of course land and other realty hold the first place, and live stock the second.

The six thousand miles of railroad in Texas, at *one half* the average cost throughout the United States, would amount to $210,000,000.

By reference to the report of the Comptroller, it appears that the taxable property of the State was

In 1871	$222,504,073
In 1877	319,373,221
In 1878	303,202,426
In 1879	304,193,163
In 1880	301,470,736
In 1881	375,000,000
In 1882	419,927,476
In 1883	527,537,390
In 1884	603,060,917*

In 1870 there was less than 300 miles of railroad in the State. From 1870 to 1877 there were added 1,300 miles; 400 miles were built in 1877, 200 in 1878, and 700 each in 1879 and 1880, while in 1881 there were built over 1,500 miles. Since 1881 there have been added by the completion of roads projected nearly one thousand miles more.

It will be observed that the *gains* in the wealth of the State followed the years of greatest mileage built. Was it not dependent on the increased extension of the railroad?

I know of no better criterion by which to measure the real wealth of the State—the prosperity and progress—than by the railroad earnings. The gross earnings of the Texas roads for 1883 are put down at $21,450,445. But this is a small item, a very small factor, compared with the real amount and value of the products themselves, when it is remembered that the

*See note, page 29.

freight was moved at an average cost of 1.8 cents per ton per mile; that passengers were carried for 3.5 cents per mile before the late law (3 cents) went into effect. However, passenger traffic is every where small as compared with freight, being in Texas less than a third of the gross earnings.

By a comparison of the average cost of moving a ton a mile in the several groups of States, it will be found that Texas roads are not exorbitant in their charges.

It costs in New England 1.7 cents per ton per mile; in the Middle States *one cent* per ton; in the Southern States 1.8 cents; in the Western States 1.2 cents; in the Pacific States 2.2 cents per ton per mile.

Nor is a comparison of these rates with the leading countries of Europe damaging to America. The actual cost to the companies (not what they charge for moving a ton a mile) in France is 1.7 cents; in Belgium 1.5 cents per ton per mile.

Much is heard about "The monopolies," "The soulless corporations!" I can not see where so much monopoly, so much extortion, so much discrimination comes in. That can not be very oppressive to the laboring man which transports his year's provision, for one day's labor, from Chicago to any eastern point. That can not be a discrimination against the consumer, at least, which transports from Chicago to New York seventeen barrels of flour at the rate of one mile for *one cent.* I know of no lesson so fruitful in its teachings as the reduction in railway charges made by the railroad managements themselves from 1873 to 1879. Competition, the great law governing all trades, forced this reduction, and by which carefully prepared statistics show that these corporations lost, or there was saved to the shippers — the consumers really — in the space of six years, $922,000,000 in freights alone.

I do not wish to be understood as denying the rights of legislatures, or Congress, as to the control of the traffic rates—the regulation, as it is termed, of railroads. I simply propose to state the facts—the results in two cases: The New York Central was chartered—consolidated in the face of determined opposition. Passenger-rates were fixed by law at two cents per mile. After the lapse now of twenty years the rate is still two cents a mile. The freight rates were left without regulation—the latter have been reduced from 3 cents per ton per mile to .83 of a cent a ton a mile; or the result of competition has lowered the rate to less than one third of the former rate.

The Texas & Pacific has reduced its freight from 3.34 cents per ton per mile (1877) to 1.76 cents in 1883, a reduction of nearly one half. Here is a fruitful study for the political mathematician—the legislative accountant.

When the legislature of Texas reduced the passenger fare from five to three cents per mile, I was met by the Hon. John Hancock, now a member of Congress from this State, and addressed thus:

"Professor, I understand you say that while the passenger'gets the benefit of 40 per cent reduction, that the railroads have really lost 66⅔ per cent. I do not see this." Said I: "Do you see the first?" "Yes," said he. I asked, "What part of *three* must you add to make the result five?" Said he, "Two thirds." "That is," said I, "the roads must now carry *five* passengers at three cents to realize the same that they did for carrying *three* passengers at *five* cents. Or," said I, "to be more practical, hold up your five fingers; turn *two* down—two fifths off. Now, return from *three* to five, add two, turn the same two up; *two thirds* of three this time." "I see it," said he; "You shall have the chair of mathematics in our university."

In this same legislative discussion another fallacy—a very grave mistake—was made by these legislative accountants. It was contended that since the New York Central carried passengers for *two* cents a mile, the Texas roads could certainly do it for three—that the reduction of the rate would more than double the amount of travel—that people would travel simply to travel!

Another comparison: The New York Central has not quite 1,000 miles of main track (953). In 1883 this road carried 10,746,925 passengers. Since a proportion is a comparison, "If 1,000 miles carry 11,276,930, how many should 6,000 miles carry?" Answer, 67,661,580; or, according to our last census, more than *forty-two* times the entire population of Texas—that is every man, woman, and child—would have to make forty-two trips each to put the roads of Texas upon the same basis as the New York Central.

The facts show that the results of legislative restrictions have maintained *maximum* rates, while without these restrictions the tendency to lower rates has been the uniform rule.

Killing the goose that lays the golden egg is not quite the fable to which I would point our legislative regulators, but I would remind them of the fate of Cadmus endeavoring to rescue his sister Europa, carried off by Jupiter, that while he destroyed the dreadful serpent, that going still further, following the advice of Minerva, he sowed the teeth of the dragon, which immediately springing up as armed men destroyed each other, Cadmus himself not being exempt from the terrible catastrophe.

"The discriminations," as they are termed, between local and through rates, are the same that are hourly met with between the retail and wholesale dealers in our towns as well as cities.

The railroad managements "do discriminate," and always in favor of the press and the pulpit. A prominent minister of one of our leading denominations told me he had ridden free, in one year, 24,640 miles upon the various roads of Texas—over 5,000 miles being upon the lines of a single company.* Hundreds of other ministers can testify to this same liberality of these same corporations toward the spread of the Gospel. The Texas roads keep a temperance lecturer continually traveling over the State, free as to transportation, to wage a ceaseless war against intemperance.

One of our greatest General Managers says: "At all times put me down, first, in favor of public free schools; second, and under all circumstances, against whisky." If temperance legislation would go as far as railroad managers, soon we would be rid of drunkenness. Gradually, slowly, if you choose, but they are coming to it. The general orders are beginning to read, "No man who uses intoxicating liquors will be retained in the employ of this company."

This year orders have been issued prohibiting the use of intoxicating liquors *off* as well as *on* duty, on the whole Missouri Pacific system. It has been the standing order of the Baltimore & Ohio and other roads for years.

The next step will be to prohibit the use of tobacco; a narcotic only, it

---

*This is not at all improbable. John Morriss, a conductor upon the Texas & Pacific, made, around *"The Quadrantal,"* 61,732 miles in one year, was in Ft. Worth every day, and "in bed every night," with the usual "lay-overs."   2

is true, but to the habitual user is next in its deleterious influence to whisky.

The railroads will regulate themselves—are doing it every day. There are many things about them I would like to see changed; there are many things they would change themselves, and they themselves will change them.

There is also a growing apprehension, a needless alarm upon the part of the people, as to the increasing power of the railroads. Fears are expressed that they will control the government—not for good, but for evil.

The recent introduction of steam as a road motive-power (in this country not till 1830), the rapid progress of railroad construction, and the length of the lines operated—122,000 miles—the immense values that are represented, $6,500,000,000 (*six thousand five hundred millions of dollars*), one eighth of the aggregate values of all kinds of property in the Union—all these, with the changed conditions wrought by them, have had much to do in creating this alarm. But this has reference to our own country only. The lines of railroads in the five divisions of the earth, according to Baron Kolb, cost *sixteen billions* of dollars, and will reach *eight* times around the globe. And all this has been brought about in a little over a half century.*

If Britannia ruled the seas through her ships, why not Columbia rule the continents through her locomotives?

We do not hear that the mother-country ever used her navy to oppress her own people; why fear that the daughter will use her railroads to mar her own beauty or to defeat her own greatness?

I say, "The railroad is solving commercial and social problems—is the greatest pioneer, the greatest missionary ever sent out by Church or State."

I have fully sustained the first propositions. I said, in 1880, to *The National Teachers' Association*, a body of thinkers not surpassed in this or any other country:

"*I believe the whistle of the Texas & Pacific locomotives will carry our civilization, our enterprise, our religion, and our language into the rocky Sierra Nevadas, until not only Mexico, but from the lakes to the gulf, and from ocean to ocean will be ours, and that, too, without a battle flag.*"

---

*The first railway worked by steam was opened between Darlington and Stockton, September 25, 1825.

During the past three years the American railroad has been pushing on, is invading quietly, peacefully, successfully, the capital of the Montezumas. The commission proposed by a member of Congress from Texas, only a year ago, "To cultivate amicable and commercial relations with the countries in Central and South America," is actively about its mission of Peace —Good Will.

The time is not far distant—"it is only a question of time"—when we shall realize Columbus' grand conception, a passage to the East Indies by sailing west—indeed much more than Columbus ever dreamed of—for the American railroad builders, extending their efforts, pushing their lines south, and north, into Central, into South America, into Alaska, crossing Behring

Straits (only twenty-six miles wide) in a steamer, will thus connect by a continuous and unbroken highway all the continents; will bind, will unite by this great commercial artery the interests of Chili and Brazil with Japan and China, New York, San Francisco and Yukon with Moscow and St. Petersburg.

Byron wrote, little more than half a century ago:

> "But every mountain now hath found a tongue,
> And Jura answers through her misty shroud,
> Back to the joyous Alps, who call to her aloud."

To-day, were he living, he would realize his prophecy fulfilled; he would hear, and in his dear mother-tongue, not only amid Alpine heights, but upon every plain in Europe and Asia:

"ALL RIGHT?"   "GO AHEAD!"

A clever Modern Philologist shows that the English language is spoken to-day by 100,000.000 of people, that soon—within a hundred years—will be the language of 1,000,000,000 (one thousand million) souls; adds, that then the great languages of the world will be the English, Chinese, and Russian, with the English far in the lead. But he does not tell us to what influence this wonderful spread of our language—this universality of our mother-tongue—is due. He does not tell why Europe was—is to day—a *Babel.* He does not tell us that steam and electricity, iron and steel, have enabled this people to subdue, to possess the earth this side the Atlantic. He does not tell us that the echoes and re-echoes of the steam-whistle were not heard resounding through the corridors of the Alps till late this century!

Mr. Webster was a great admirer of the mother-country, especially of her territorial acquisitions, her military glory, and in one of his grandest and loftiest flights of imagination, describing the progress and prowess, the greatness and extent, of the British nation, said: "It is a power which has dotted the face of the whole globe all over with her possessions and military posts, whose morning drum-beat, following the sun and keeping company with the hours, circles the earth daily with one continuous and unbroken strain of the martial airs of England."

It delights me—it thrills me—to think upon my country, my people, and my language! Could the immortals, could Jefferson, the "author of the Declaration," could Washington, "the father of his country," look out from their celestial abode, they would behold to-day our FREE REPUBLIC (stretching through more than one hundred and eighty degrees of longitude), all dotted over with school-houses and colleges and churches, whose rising-bells and morning prayer-calls and evening hymns, following the sun in his course and keeping company with the hours, fill the air daily with the merry laugh and joyous shout and happy song of a continuous and unbroken continent of ENGLISH-SPEAKING PEOPLE!

The solution? The White Sails of Commerce brought this blue-eyed, fair-skinned, light-haired race to our shores, the Locomotive carried into the interior the messengers of peace, and in their tracks followed smiling Plenty, with her attendant hand-maids, Religious Liberty, Political Freedom, and Universal Education.

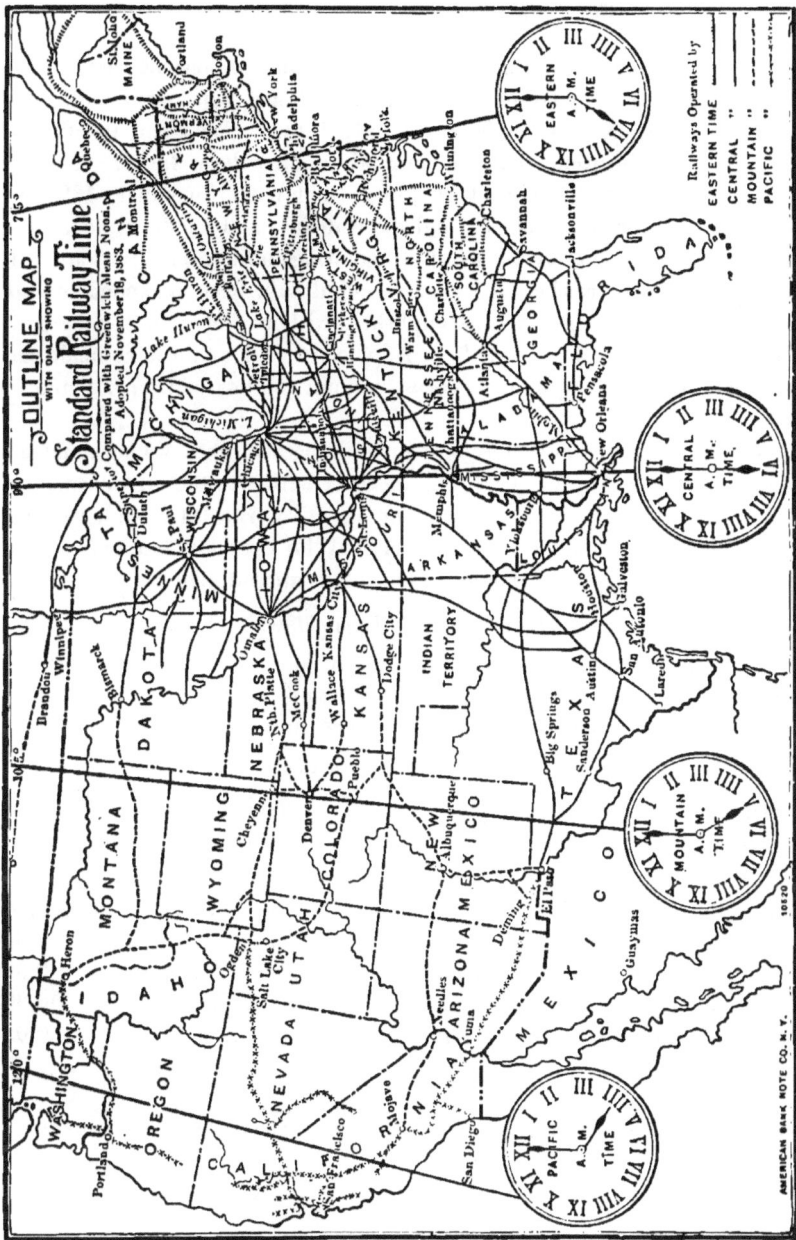

OUTLINE MAP
WITH DIALS SHOWING
Standard Railway Time
As Compared with Greenwich Mean Noon,
Adopted November 18, 1883.

EASTERN A.M. TIME

CENTRAL A.M. TIME

MOUNTAIN A.M. TIME

PACIFIC A.M. TIME

Railways Operated by
EASTERN TIME
CENTRAL "
MOUNTAIN "
PACIFIC "

AMERICAN BANK NOTE CO. N.Y.

I address to-day scientific men of the leading nations of earth. You can bear witness of your efforts, your resolutions, your arguments, your logic, your reasons to bring about standard time. You can testify, too, with some mortification, that all your labors have been futile. Yet, you have learned. I tell you that on the 18th day of November, 1883, the clocks of 20,000 railroad offices, and the watches of 300,000 employes were reset—the minute and second hands all pointing to the same division on the *dial*—that the people who did the same could have been reckoned by millions; and that all this was accomplished without delay to commerce or injury to person. No general, from Napoleon down, could have made such a change, even in a single army corps, without the loss of property and life too.[*]

Again, who have been foremost in building churches, schools, and colleges, in endowing universities, and in contributing to the advancement of liberal, higher education? Where can it be so truthfully said, "charity never faileth," as among railroad men? Who ever knew a real case of charity turned from office, home, or tent of a railroad man?

Charity: " '*Tis mightiest in the mightiest.*"

America's great Triumvirate in action, in the successful completion, control, and management of the three great trunk railways of our country, abounded in good works, in large beneficence, and

"Their deeds do follow them."

In addition to many smaller, but no less valuable charities, Col. Thomas A. Scott, just before his death, gave the following amounts to the following institutions :

To Jefferson Medical College, of Philadelphia................................. $50,000
To the Orthopædic Hospital, of Philadelphia............................. 30,000
To Children's Department of Episcopal Hospital, of Philadelphia.. 20,000
To University of Pennsylvania, of Philadelphia....................... 50,000
To Washington and Lee University, of Virginia....................... 50,000

  Total.. 200,000

[*] Mr. Wm. F. Allen, of the Traveler's Guide, is the author of Standard Time. The next move will be to the Single Dial for the day, to 24 o'clock : "Train No. 1 will meet No. 2 at Station No. III, at 17.17 (o clock)."

In regard to the numerous gifts of father and son—the Vanderbilts—I do not know how better to present the same than by giving the letter of the Chancellor of the Vanderbilt University, Bishop H. N. McTyeire.

NASHVILLE, TENN., Jan. 29, 1885.
MY DEAR PROFESSOR:

I thank you for your letter. . . . . Mr. Cornelius (Commodore) Vanderbilt gave this University one million of dollars. Of that sum we have now as invested endowment, bearing seven per cent per annum, $600.000. His son, Mr. Wm. H. Vanderbilt, since his father's death, has given to Vanderbilt University $250,000; and a $100,000 of this sum has been added to our endowment. Generous benefactors to the South and to general education!

The location of Vanderbilt University has made Nashville what they call "The Athens of the South." Others have come here since.

I believe our catalogue this year will show students from twenty States and Territories, all accessible to *railroads*.

In honor of our donors we give marked attention to civil engineering, including the theoretical and practical knowledge of building *railroads*. We believe in railroads with good cause.

For mounting and equipping the observatory for the Leander McCormick telescope Mr. Wm. H. Vanderbilt gave $25,000 to the Virginia University.

Last year he gave $500,000 to the College of Physicians and Surgeons, of the city of New York. These two, father and son, gave for the purposes enumerated, *one million five hundred and twenty-five thousand dollars*.

But additionally, and in purpose and result too—a greater gift still—Mr. Wm. H. Vanderbilt has given $150,000 to establish at Washington a Museum of Patriotism, where the collections, the offerings and trophies, the honors paid General Grant by the nations of the earth are to be perpetually preserved for the inspection and admiration of all American youth, and that through all future generations.

Or in the aggregate, Mr. Wm. H. Vanderbilt alone has contributed to schools of science, schools of medicine, and a school of patriotism, *nine hundred and twenty-five thousand dollars*.

* He is still in the prime of life, full of vigor, abounding in good deeds, and it may reasonably be expected that he will yet outstrip his father's great work, the founding and equipping of the Vanderbilt University.

* See note, page 30.

Col. John W. Garrett leaves the following, greater than either of his associates in extent and in security of investment. These annuities represent a basis of over a *million dollars* ($1,100,000) at six and five per cent.

The clauses of the will pertaining to these gifts and their purposes seem to be worthy of reprinting, even in so short an address as this :

And upon the further trust that my said trustees shall, from the stocks and bonds belonging to my estate, select such good interest-bearing securities as shall amount to the sum of one hundred thousand dollars, or in their option invest the sum of one hundred thousand dollars of the moneys belonging to my estate in such manner as to produce the yearly sum of six thousand dollars, which said sum I desire shall be paid yearly to aid in improving the condition of the poor in the city of Baltimore, the first payment to be made at the expiration of one year from my death, and to continue thereafter in perpetuity; and as I have a very favorable opinion of the usefulness and effectiveness of the present organization or body corporate known as the "Baltimore Association for the Improvement of the Condition of the Poor," I recommend my said trustees, so long as in their judgment this charitable institution is efficiently managed, to give said sum of six thousand dollars to the said association annually for the purposes aforesaid; and if at any future period, in the judgment of my said trustees, said sum of six thousand dollars per year can be applied or distributed so as to confer greater benefit upon the poor of Baltimore, in that event I direct my said trustees so in their discretion to apply said sum.

And upon the further trust out of the net income of any estate to devote the sum of fifty thousand dollars annually to such objects of benevolence, to educational purposes, to aid virtuous and struggling persons, and to such works of public utility as are calculated to promote the happiness, usefulness, and progress of society; said amount of fifty thousand dollars per annum to be apportioned to the furtherance of such objects and to the accomplishment of such ends in the judgment and at the discretion of my trustees, it is my will, and I so direct that the contributions to the purposes named in this clause shall continue during the lifetime of my children, Robert Garrett, Thomas Harrison Garrett, and Mary Elizabeth Garrett, and of the survivors and survivor of them, and that the same shall be continued thereafter by their heirs if the condition of the estate will then justify the said appropriation. I desire that the contributions and assistance to be given under this clause of my will shall, as far as practicable, be devoted to the promotion of the objects herein named in the city of Baltimore and in the State of Maryland; but in case of special suffering or distress in other communities, my trustees shall have the power to use their discretion and judgment in relieving the same.

From a personal friend to the two benefactors I learn that Mr. Garrett really directed the gifts of Mr. Johns Hopkins. Mr. Garrett is reported as having said: "Johns, give while you live, so that you may direct and see the fruits of your labors."

Johns did give while living, and the Johns Hopkins University is the result of the accumulated efforts of Mr. Hopkins, much of this being "the earnings" of his stock in the Baltimore & Ohio Railroad. The latter road during the lifetime of Mr. Garrett was proverbial for the care of its employes. The Baltimore & Ohio Relief Association, furnishing all the advantages of a mutual life insurance company, a savings bank, and a building association, was peculiarly the result of Mr. Garrett's forethought, and the pride of his administration.

The company has announced the organization of a School of Technology for the training of young men—the future employes of the company. This school, located at Mount Clare (Baltimore), will be formally opened September next. The object and the purpose of this institution will be to give the Baltimore & Ohio a force of trained men, those having the advantages of a suitable amount of literary instruction as well as that practical teaching which they will most need.*

I must add here, for the sentiment, for the lofty and manly and elevating spirit of the donor, the following. Said Mr. George I. Seney: "If any one asks you why I have given so much money to the Wesleyan Female College, of Georgia, tell them it was to honor my mother, to whom, under God, I owe more than to all the world besides."

Mr. Seney gave to the Wesleyan Female College and to Emory College, of Georgia, $450,000.†

Mrs. Leland Stanford, since the spirit of her dear boy has departed (*abiit non periit*), has organized, in the city of San Francisco, four Kindergarten schools, locating them in those portions of the city most destitute, and has dedicated them to the motherless and homeless little ones of her great and lowly, her splendid and yet shadowy city.‡

Already has this benefactress, if not repaid, been compensated in her affliction for her loss. A mother writes her: "My children shall be taught to love Leland's memory, follow his example, and imitate his lovely character."

* See note, page 33.   † See note, page 33.   ‡ See note, page 31.

The ex-Governor, it is said, contemplates—has determined that Palo Alto, "the beautiful, sweet Palo Alto," of the boy, shall be the site of Leland's University.

Those who know the father, his liberal culture, his broad views, and his entire acquaintance with all the educational systems and institutions of learning at home and abroad, being a personal friend of many of the savants of Europe, with an abundance of means at his command, know that this will be a real university, surpassing the English universities and leading those on the Continent, since it will deal with the practical, living issues of all science, social, political, and physical.

There will be, too, a liberality toward the distinguished scholars called to these appointments—their services in their specialties will be *specially* rewarded. The man who pays the trainers of his horses more at present in wages and perquisites than his State University pays her professors will evidently pay to the conductors of the various departments of this university, founded and named to honor his only child, salaries commensurate with the founder's appreciation of mind over matter.*

Mr. President, I have seen much of this Continent, have seen more of Texas. That which in our school geographies was called "The American Desert"—later, "The Staked Plains"—is no desert at all. Since the building of the Texas & Pacific this vast area has become (was all the time) fertile. All the cereals grow luxuriantly. Pure water, and in abundance, is found all over, throughout these plains, costs but the digging of a shallow well. Here, sir, is so happily, so truthfully verified the great promise, that not only " *The wilderness and solitary places shall be glad for them* " (the railroads), but " *The desert shall rejoice and blossom as the rose,*" that I venture to suggest—I assert, Africa is not Africa because it is the home of the colored man ; but the colored man is the colored man because his home is in Africa! Needs but the touch of Ithuriel's spear, the life-giving breath, the awakening influences of the locomotive, and this "Dark Continent," this land of Ham, will take its rightful place in the brotherhood of Shem and Japheth, all then being of one speech and one language, and *that* the Anglo-Saxon.

But, sir, I must close, and yet I can not do so without adding one other reflection. A few days ago, standing upon the track of the Texas & Pacific, and turning my eyes east and west, surveying its long line of 1,487 miles

*See note, page 34.

traversing the most fertile portions of the territory of Texas, connecting the waters of each ocean, I was forced to the conviction that, for many miles on either side, there will be presented a phenomenon not unlike the gulf stream, except that the warm waters of the latter will be replaced by the warm hearts of an intelligent, enterprising, and thrifty population.

Some will select the fertile prairies, others will dwell amid the sierras, in search of the rich placers, while others still will be content to tend their flocks and count their herds.

Of these and those who shall come after them there will be an unbroken (life-blood) current from the Pacific to the Atlantic and from the Atlantic to the Pacific, for this will truly be the highway of nations.

Sir, it is said that the ancients never worshipped the setting sun. This is more than true of our own modern devotees. Still it would be remissness, indeed, upon my part, to close this address without asking the question, to whose statesmanship, to whose forethought, to whose prophetic ken was due this gigantic enterprise, this girdling the continent, uniting ocean with ocean?

Moving west, still west, and yet still west, pausing in front and at the very base of rugged and awe-crowned Sierra Blanca, said I, "A hundred thousand years hast thou stood sentinel over this vast valley and plain—long hast thou guarded this Pass; mayst thou yet stand a thousand thousand years, witnessing daily the transformations, 'the sweet influences,' of the peaceful locomotive, and adding perpetually thy testimony to the sagacity of the originator of the project 'to build a railroad on or near the thirty-second parallel of latitude.'"

Monuments and mausoleums, bronze and brass, may fitly commemorate the deeds of dead heroes, so styled by the world, amid the glare and glitter, the flush and flurry of the battle-field, but the long lines of this road, stretching across this united continent, bearing the trains heavily freighted with the rich returns of honest toil, will ever be the most appropriate monument to the wisdom and skill of the builders and present managers—while perennially the flower-decked prairie will add its fragrance to and forever embalm the memory of Thomas A. Scott, the great projector of the Texas & Pacific Railway Company.

ADDENDA.

NOTE A.

Since the delivery and the publication (1885) of *The Railroad in Education* many changes have taken place—important economical results have been reached—beneficial to the country, because cheapening the cost of transportation.

Says Mr. Edward Atkinson:

"The New York Central and Hudson River Railroad may be taken as a good example of an important line of railroad under most efficient management, and as a standard of what all other lines may accomplish when the magnitude of their traffic will permit them to make as great a reduction in rates. The average charge per ton per mile on this line from 1865 to 1868, four years, was 3.0097 cents per ton per mile. From 1882 to 1885, four years, the charge was 0.7895. Difference 2.2202 cents

"If we may assume that the people of the United States have been saved two and one fifth cents per ton per mile on the whole railway traffic of the last four years, either from the construction of railways where none before existed, or by such a reduction in the charge for their service, the amount of money's worth saved in four years has been $3,898,373,159, which sum would probably equal the cash cost of all the railways built in the United States since 1865, to which sum may probably be added the entire payment upon the national debt since 1865."

Or, these conditions fulfilled, there has been enough saved in transportation alone in the short space of four years to give every man, woman, and child in the United States $77.70 apiece.

But to what is this great reduction due? How has this revolution on freight charges been brought about? Simply by the invariable and consistent law of commerce, a *non*-commissioned regulation.

(28)

Note B.

Taxable property in 1885.................................... $621,011,989
Taxable property in 1886.................................... ... 630,525,123

As observed, the gains in the wealth of the State have followed the years of active railroad building.

During the years 1885 and 1886 there was added to the mileage of Texas nearly an equal amount each year, aggregating 1,234 miles, or swelling the total railway system, beginning 1887, to 7,234 miles; placing Texas as the sixth State in the Union in regard to railroads. Illinois, Iowa, Pennsylvania, New York, and Ohio, in this grouping lie immediately above her, Illinois being the highest, with 9,579 miles.

This year, 1887, gives evidence so far as being a year of greater activity than both the preceding, and hence an increased taxable value largely over 1886 may be confidently anticipated. Texas should have for her full development double the present mileage; indeed, to put her upon the same footing as Illinois, she should have over 40,000 miles—should have really 44,444.

Illinois has at present a mile of railroad to every 321 inhabitants; Texas a mile to every 277. But the area of Texas—the territory to be traversed is *five times* as great as that of Illinois; hence capitalists need not hesitate about "occupying the ground." There is still room for investment in railroad building in Texas.

In 1878 I prepared, and published in 1879,

Industrial Education—(Origin and Progress).

In this pamphlet will be found:

"Wheat is one of the chief staples of Texas. Fully peopled and fully developed, Texas can furnish for exportation for the markets of the world 64,000,000 bushels of wheat, can furnish more than is now furnished by the United States, Russia, and Austria combined. 'Fully developed' is the talismanic word. But that this may be shown to be within bounds, has been actually done, I cite but a single case: France, less in area than Texas, in 1869 produced 297,000,000 bushels of wheat, or 67,000,000 bushels more than the whole United States, as given by the census of 1870."

This year Mr. Edward Atkinson, eminent authority on all statistics, says:

" The entire wheat crop of the United States could be grown on wheat land of the best quality selected from that part of the area of the State of Texas by which that single State exceeds the present area of the German Empire."

The German Empire has only 8,000 square miles more than France. Again says Mr. Atkinson:

" The cotton factories of the world now require about 12,000,000 bales of cotton of American weight. Good land in Texas produces one bale to an acre. The world's supply of cotton could therefore be grown on less than 19,000 square miles, or upon an area equal to only seven per cent of the area of Texas."

Note C.

Contrary to our then reasonable expectations Mr. Wm. H. Vanderbilt on the 8th of December, 1885, was stricken down, really " in the prime of life" and " full of vigor."

The shock with which his immediate friends received the news of his death is the best evidence of how unexpected it was, while the tribute of these same friends closely associated with him is given as the best exponent of the life and character of the man.

" His sudden death, in the very midst of the activities whose influence reached over the continent, has startled the whole country, and in the hush of strife and passions the press and public give tender sympathy to the bereaved family, and pay just and deserving tribute to his memory. But to us who were his associates and friends, endeared to him by the strongest ties and years of intimacy, the event is an appalling calamity, full of sorrow and the profoundest sense of personal loss; while officially we feel that his sagacity, his strong common sense, his thorough knowledge of the business, his willingness to lend his vast resources in times of peril, and his counsel and assistance were of invaluable and incalculable service in conducting and sustaining these great enterprises.

" He came into the possession of the largest estate ever devised to a single individual, and has administered the great trust with modesty, without arrogance, and with generosity. He never used his riches as a means of oppression, or to destroy or injure the enterprises or business of others, but it constantly flowed into the enlargement of old and the construction and development of new works, semi-public in their character, which opened new avenues of local and national wealth, and gave opportunity and employment directly and indirectly to millions of people. To the employes of his railroads he was exacting in discipline and the performance of duty. He was merciless to negligence or bad habits in a vocation where millions of lives were dependent upon alertness and fidelity. But within these limits he was a just and generous employer and superior officer. He knew how to reward faithfulness and remember good conduct, and always held the respect and allegiance of the vast bodies of men who called him chief. With all the temptations which surround unlimited wealth his home-life was simple, and no happier domestic circle could any where be found. The loved companion with whom he began his active life in the first dawn of his manhood was his help, comfort, and happiness through all his career, and his children have one and all honored their father and their mother, and taken the places which they worthily fill in their several spheres of activity and usefulness."

As an evidence of the direction given by the example of the family, grandfather and father, we find the following, and in behalf of and for the benefit of the same employes, that a social school, with halls and libraries and even home comforts is provided by CORNELIUS:

"As an outgrowth of this work the Young Men's Christian Association, and because of the felt need of larger and better accommodations, Mr. Vanderbilt, on the 30th of June, made a proposition to the Board of Directors of the New York Central Railroad, that if they would set apart a plot of land eighty by forty feet, on the corner of Forty-fifth Street and Madison Avenue as a site for a building to be used by the railroad men centering at the Grand Central Depot, he would at his own expense erect thereon a magnificent building, adapted in all respects to the growing demands of the work of the society with whose progress and development he was so familiar."

The proposition was accepted on behalf of the company in an appropriate and characteristic letter by President Depew, who said, among other things :

"Individually I am deeply sensible that this work will lighten the burdens of the administration of the affairs of the company, and promote that good feeling and mutual and interdependent interest between the executive and all departments of our business, which, increasing with years, will furnish more acceptable service to the public and add to the value of the property."

Ground was broken for the new building 1st September, 1886. When finished it will contain, on the first floor, reception-room, offices and committee rooms, reading-room and library containing 7,000 volumes, and a room for games. In the basement will be located the gymnasium and bowling alleys, bath rooms of the most modern kind, including a large plunge, and a boiler for heating the building. The second floor will be devoted to the large hall for lectures, concerts, and other entertainments, and will contain rooms for classes; and on the third floor quarters will be provided for the janitor, while in the upper story provisions will be made for men to sleep who occasionally remain in the city over night. The building will be of brick, trimmed with terra cotta, and the interior finished in the most handsome and modern style.

Turning from the provision completed for the comforts of the working classes, and of his employment, Mr. Vanderbilt contributes to the promotion of taste and a love of the fine arts, presenting to the Metropolitan Museum of Art, in New York City, the painting by Rosa Bonheur, entitled "The Horse Fair," purchased at the sale of the Stewart collection at a cost of $53,000. His reason for this presentation is best given in his own words:

"It seems to me to be a work of art which should be in a position where it can permanently be accessible to the public. In the gallery of the Museum this object will be attained."

An appreciative public, as these facts become known, must forget the millionaire in their admiration of the man.

Note D.

Has it not been established that good deeds are hereditary—are transmitted from father to son? The school established at Mont Clare, at a cost to the Baltimore & Ohio of $25,000, has been by the company voted an annual appropriation for its support of $20,000.

Soon this, for the employes, is followed by a gift of $8,000 by the President, Mr. Robert Garrett, to "The New Art Museum" of Princeton College.

Thus again is exhibited the broad philanthropy of the benefactor, suitably contributing to the needs of one, as well as to the tastes of another class of persons.

Note E.

While Mr. Seney was making an outright gift of $450,000 to Emory, and the Wesleyan Female College, (ex-Governor) Senator Joseph E. Brown, the President of "The Western & Atlantic Railroad," was purchasing in the market bonds of the State of Georgia belonging to the University, in order to establish a perpetual fund to aid in educating indigent young men, by a loan on certain easy conditions.

The number benefited now, from twenty to twenty five, will increase annually.

This is not a donation; the beneficiaries agree to pay back the amount received with 4 per cent interest, the main idea being to help those who make an effort to help themselves.

The original fund was $50,000, bearing seven per cent interest.

This gift, or loan rather, is known as " The Charles McDonald Brown Scholarship Fund."

The real object and scope of this fund is best given in the language of the sagacious donor :

" The object is to help indigent young men who are poor and promising and who are not able to help themselves, and who have not friends able to help them. The

3

terms of the donation do not permit any young man to receive more than two hundred dollars per annum for his expenses while at college. The tuition is free, and where a young man has one hundred dollars per annum, or can command that, he is permitted to have an additional hundred to help out and enable him to finish his education when he could not otherwise do it.

"The same is true, whether the amount he can furnish be more or less than one hundred dollars, as he would be allowed to receive the benefit of the fund to the extent of the balance necessary to make up the two hundred dollars per annum. The object here, as they are poor boys, is not to put it in their reach to be extravagant, but to compel them to get along on two hundred a year, their tuition being free, which they can do and live comfortably."

Provision is made for a system of competitive examinations, where they can be had, which are reported from the different counties, and upon these reports the trustees of the University make up their decision as to who is most entitled.

Within less than a half century the rich fruits of this scholarship will be observed in the field and forum, in the workshop and in the counting house, in all the peaceful, productive walks of life of the great empire State of Georgia.

Note F.

The four kindergarten schools have grown into eight, with an attendance of over six hundred children. Mrs. Stanford bears the entire expense, receiving as a grateful compensation that many mothers now write her:

"'My children shall be taught to love Leland's memory, follow his example, and imitate his lovely character.'"

Note G.

"His liberal culture, his broad views, and an abundance of means at his command," have enabled the Governor to name a Board of Control for

"Leland's University." Thirty millions of property has been designated as the foundation of this school.

The design of it is truly to "deal with the practical living issues of all science, social, political, and physical." Article I of the grant sets forth:

"The Nature, Object, and Purposes of the Institution hereby founded to be:

"Its nature, that of a University, with such seminaries of learning as shall make it of the highest grade, including mechanical institutes, museums, galleries of art, laboratories and conservatories, together with all things necessary for the study of agriculture in all its branches, and for mechanical training, and the studies and exercises directed to the cultivation and enlargement of the mind.

"Its object, to qualify its students for personal success and direct usefulness in life.

"And its purposes, to promote the public welfare by exercising an influence in behalf of humanity and civilization, teaching the blessings of liberty regulated by law, and inculcating love and reverence for the great principles of government as derived from the inalienable rights of man to life, liberty, and the pursuit of happiness."

"ARTICLE IV.

"POWERS AND DUTIES OF THE TRUSTEES.

"SECTION 9. To appoint a President of the University, who shall not be one of their number, and to remove him at will.

"SEC. 10. To employ professors and teachers at the University.

"SEC. 11. To fix the salaries of the president, professors, and teachers, and to fix them at such rates as will secure to the University the services of men of the very highest attainment.

"SEC. 14. To prohibit sectarian instruction, but to have taught in the University the immortality of the soul, the existence of an all-wise and benevolent Creator, and that obedience to His laws is the highest duty of man."

Do not these quotations justify the prediction of 1885: "There will be, too, a liberality toward the distinguished scholars called to these appointments—their services in their specialties will be *specially* rewarded. The man who pays the trainers of his horses more at present in wages and perquisites than his State University pays her professors will evidently pay to the conductors of the various departments of this University, founded and named to honor his only child, salaries commensurate with the founder's appreciation of mind over matter."

One other remarkable fact about this grant, that while our endowments for colleges and universities have been usually the gifts of either a man or woman singly, this is the joint-grant of:

" We, Leland Stanford and Jane Lathrop Stanford, husband and wife, grantors, desiring to promote the public welfare by founding, endowing, and having maintained upon our estate, known as the Palo Alto Farm, etc."

The foundations have been laid:

"MENLO PARK, CAL., May 15th.—The corner-stone of the first building of the Leland Stanford, jr., University was laid this morning at Palo Alto."

NOTE H.

WORK AND WEALTH.

These are not the same—they are not "equals"—they are mathematical "equivalents."

Work is the cause, wealth the result—work the instrument, wealth the effect—work the procuring agent, wealth the accumulated product:

"As unto the bow the cord is,"

So is work unto wealth,

" Useless each without the other."

And while by no amount of discussion can work and wealth be shown to be the same, it is equally true, however, that there must be peace—harmony between them.

Work is most effective, most productive when it is "sustained" and " protected" by wealth.

This position presupposes organization, and there is as much reason for organization among working men as among moneyed men—but this organization must be in the direction of doing, not in the prevention of doing.

Hence " the strike " is wrong in theory and doubly so in practice. In

practice it not only requires the withdrawal of certain individuals from
work but prevents others from working.

While it may not be so easy to establish the position, that no one has a
right, in health, to quit work, it can easily be shown that the prevention of
others is clearly wrong and a direct interference with personal liberty.

"This is theory!" says one.

Take an example of the late strike in the Southwest; take the evidence
of disinterested and also of interested sources:

"The loss to the Missouri Pacific Railway through last year's strike is placed in
the annual report of the company at $500,000, while the losses to the strikers are
estimated at $900,000, making a total of $1,400,000.

"THE CURTIN CONGRESSIONAL COMMITTEE."

Mr. Martin Irons, a conspicuous leader at the time of these men, says:

"Of the 4,800 engaged in this strike, there are 4,000 of them to-day without lucrative employment."

The loss here stands in the relation of *five* to *nine*—wealth coming out
"ahead" nearly as two to one, but the country—the whole people—with an
aggregate destruction of $1,400,000 of productive values—a shortage of the
actual necessaries of life to this amount.

The remedy for these troubles can not be discussed here.

The want of harmony, of entire cordiality between work and wealth, has
had its origin of late in this country in the results of the civil war.

Prices of every thing for whatever purpose became fabulously high during
the war. The demand was far greater than the supply.

The war ended and a return to normal conditions, not suddenly even, but
a tendency continually in this direction, wrought a change in the demands.
The increased and increasing number of working men with a less and less
demand for them, even at lower wages, has brought about a feeling of un-
rest—a spirit of discontent. The idea has become prevalent that the poor
(the working man) has become poorer, because he gets less for his same
work, forgetting the fact that he can purchase more with the same amount
of money; and that the rich (wealthy man) has become richer, which again
is not the fact, it is only an aggregation of the riches, wealth of many men,
controlled, it may be, by one man.

456692

And as the railroad corporations seem to have gotten this control in long lines, accumulated wealth, they have been attacked as the common enemy of the poor man.

It is true these lines have been lengthened, and these corporations have become larger, and immense amounts of money have been *invested* in them, not realized or made by them—so much that they have attracted the criticisms and provoked the envy of the discontented, receiving at the same time the denunciations of a large number of people who ought to know better the actual situation.

As compared with other aggregations of wealth the railroad should be ranked high, and the accumulation of vast properties, franchises, and even privileges should be readily conceded to these corporations. For the whole economy of nature and art is comprised under these three heads: Transmutation, Transformation, and Transportation.

The former is chemical, the second mechanical, and the third, that which deals with the products ready for the use of man, comes under and justly belongs to the transporting power, whether by sail or steam, whether on water or land.

The activity of railroad building lately has been the salvation of the farmer and mechanic—has been a means of distributing this accumulated wealth that would have been forever "hoarded" but for them. This is especially true of the South: railroads have been built far in advance of the demand for them, and years must elapse before they reach even an expense basis, much less a "dividend-declaring" basis, having penetrated far into the unpeopled sections in order to provide for the approach of the coming settler.

These same railroads, all along their lines, are boring for water, demonstrating the fact, or putting beyond experiment the question that an abundance of the purest water can be obtained all across what have heretofore been reckoned barren plains. These railroads are doing all this for the benefit of the new citizen, who with his small means can not afford to incur the expense of such investigation.

There is a strange inconsistency in the action of the men who are without railroads and those who have them. The former work for their location, talk for them, and even pay money in subsidy to secure them; the latter abuse them as monopolies, as oppressors of the poor.

There never has been a field in which the poor man (the working man) has had such a chance to come to the front as in the building, the equipping, and the managing of railroads. Neither the forum, nor the legislative hall, nor the battle-field has ever offered such opportunities to men, whose energies have been directed by their brains, as the railway service.

COMPARISONS NOT ODIOUS.

On page fifteen of this address occurs the following :

" That can not be very oppressive to the laboring man which transports his year's provisions, for one day's labor, from Chicago to any Eastern point. That can not be a discrimination against the consumer, at least, which transports from Chicago to New York seventeen barrels of flour at the rate of one mile for *one cent.*"

Convert a barrel of

FLOUR INTO BREAD.

A \$7 barrel of flour will make one hundred and eighty loaves of bread. At ten cents a loaf, the estimated cost of converting this barrel of flour into one hundred and eighty loaves of bread is \$3, showing a net profit of \$8. Total charge by railroad for transporting that barrel of flour from St. Louis to New York, 40 cents.

Or the retail dealer received twenty times as much for his little manipulations as does the railroad that transports it 1,000 miles. The receiving and delivering both being an extra expense to the railroad.

BEEF.

Good beef that costs about 9 cents per pound retails at 16 cents, a profit of over 75 per cent.

Fresh beef is transported from the Western market, say Chicago to New York or Boston, for 40 cents per 100 pounds, or less than a half cent a pound. Should the consumer complain of this?

HAMS.

The average rate of freight on hams is, say 20 cents per hundred weight ; the average weight of hams about 12 pounds, or eight hams per hundred weight. That is, the freight on eight hams is about 20 cents; on a single ham, one eighth of that, or 2½ cents; gross charge by railroads, 2½ cents on the whole ham, against a profit of 4 or 5 cents on a single pound paid by the consumer. Or the freight from the Western to the Eastern cities is about *one sixtieth* of the cost of the ham.

TEA.

The average cost of tea to the consumer is 80 cents per pound. Average profit 30 cents per pound. Freight charged by the railroads for carrying this tea 1,000 miles is 45 cents per hundred weight, the profit on a *single pound* exacted from the consumer is two thirds of the gross charge by railroad for carrying 100 pounds 1,000 miles.

BOOTS AND SHOES.

The profit on a single pair of $4 boots or shoes is equal to three times the freight charges on a dozen or even twenty pair for 1,000 miles.

CLOTHING.

A good suit of clothes can be bought for $20. Weight of suit five pounds. Maximum rate for carrying this class of goods to Chicago, St. Louis, and Western points from New York, say 1,000 miles, 50 cents per hundred weight.

This suit weighs 5 pounds, 20 suits weigh 100 pounds, transportation 1,000 miles 50 cents, 2½ cents each; average profit per suit to the dealer $8. Profit to dealers 320 times the transportation.

And yet nobody complains of these profits. No regulation is discussed, no "Interstate Commerce Bill" is passed to prevent these discriminations, these monopolies. The regulation of these is left to the laws of trade, to competition, and in which the "shorter" the "haul," the larger and the "longer" this profit is exacted of the consumer, the working man.

THE INTERSTATE COMMERCE BILL.

The constitutional authority upon which this is based reads:

ARTICLE I, Section 8, Clause 3: "The Congress shall have power to regulate commerce with foreign nations, and among the several States and with the Indian tribes."

This constitution was adopted in 1787, or one hundred years ago, twenty-nine years before the first canal, thirty-two years before the first steamship crossed the Atlantic, twenty years before the Clermont ascended the Hudson, and forty-two years before a railroad, even of the rudest equipment, was constructed in this country, and hence could not have been designed to control the present railroads, or even regulate the commerce transported by them. Section 9, clause 5, of the Constitution clearly sustains this interpretation, viz., that our present Constitution never so much as anticipated railroads or their management by congressional enactment:

"No tax or duty shall be laid on articles exported from any State. No preference shall be given by any regulation of commerce or revenue to the ports of one State over those of another; nor shall vessels bound to or from one State be obliged to enter, clear or pay duties in another."

"Vessels" and "ports"—steam vessels are not even mentioned.

But that railroads as now operated should be regulated by law no one assumes to dispute. They are "public highways," "common carriers," but they are not the property of the public, they are not built by the public, not maintained by the public, and should not be controlled by the public in the sense that the navy, the army, or even a light-house is sustained.

"Rights," "privileges," "franchises," and "charters" are granted them with extraordinary powers, still their ownership, liabilities, and duties are vested in private individuals, and these should be allowed to operate them as any other business, for the profit in them.

There are scores of railroads the property wholly of one man, or family, and hence whatever may be said of their relation or duty to the public they owe no more than other individuals, or other corporations composed as they are, of individuals.

"The Interstate Commerce Bill" errs in attempting to regulate tariffs, to say at what cost certain service shall be performed, ignoring the expense of building, equipping, maintaining, and operating the several different roads, all subject to entirely different conditions. That is, in its aim to prevent discrimination it does discriminate. That while it proposes to prevent small local hardships, it entails upon the general and great public, the numberless consumers, still greater hardships, heavier freights. That the object of the bill is good no one doubts, but that it is full of difficulties, "hardships," and even in the interpretation of a wise and judicious com-

mission will take many years, with other congressional amendments and
" suspensions " to harmonize and to understand the true meaning of " Under
substantially similar circumstances and conditions."

There is still another side, and one in this era of anti-monopoly that
should not be overlooked by the statesman, nor be lost sight of by the
patriot. That when our Republic was threatened, was in the very throes of
destruction, civil war and dissolution, the Government called to its aid these
same " builders," these railroad owners and managers, to aid, to come to the
rescue, to build more roads, to bind this continent together by transcontinental railways. A net-work was soon the result. Soldiers and the mu-
nitions of war could be placed at any desired point within a few hours. The
effect of their potency and efficiency is seen to-day in an unbroken continent, one government, and a happy, united people.

The railroad during this time solved still another heretofore vexed question—the Indian question. The locomotive has been to the Indian upon
our plains what the white sails of commerce have been to the inhabitants of
the isles of the sea—THE CALUMET OF PEACE.

> "The camp has had its day of song;
>   The sword, the bayonet, the plume
> Have crowded out of rhyme too long
>   The plow, the anvil, and the loom.
> Oh! not upon our tented fields
>   Are Freedom's heroes bred alone;
> The training of the work-shop yields
>   More heroes true than war has known.
>
> " Who drives the bolt, who shapes the steel,
>   May, with a heart as valiant, strike
> As he who sees a foeman reel
>   In blood before his blow of might.
> The skill that conquers space and time,
>   That graces life, that lightens toil,
> May spring from courage more sublime
>   Than that which makes a realm its spoil."

OTHER HEROES THAN THE WORLD'S.

Some men are great in conception—some in execution—in both were

H. M. HOXIE, GEORGE NOBLE, G. J. FOREACRE.

Circumstances do not make men, neither do men make circumstances. The proper direction of circumstances makes men. And whoever becomes great in whatsoever walk of life is the man who is able to see, to grasp and direct circumstances. Such a man was H. M. Hoxie, another was George Noble, and still another was G. J. Foreacre. There were in their lives remarkable likenesses, peculiarities, contrasts, in their deaths coincidences worthy of mention here.

Mr. Hoxie died (1886) November 23d, aged fifty-six; Mr. Noble died eleven days later, December 4th, aged fifty-six, and Mr. Foreacre died December 15th, eleven days later, aged fifty-eight. However, their arduous toils, their disappointments, their successful labors, and their rich rewards can best be narrated separately.

H. M. HOXIE.

Mr. H. M. Hoxie was a native of Macedon, New York. He early in life moved to Iowa; showed in boyhood energy, decision of character, and, during the war, on account of his conspicuous ability and tact in the control and management of men, was appointed Provost Marshal of the State. In this position he performed his duties in such an impartial manner as to attract the attention of the civil as well as military officials.

When the building of the Union Pacific Railway was undertaken, Mr. Hoxie was offered a position of trust and responsibility, which he filled in such a manner as to win for himself the respect and admiration of General G. M. Dodge, the Chief Engineer, to whose brains and energy the inception and completion of the Union Pacific are mainly due.

A change in the administration of this road was brought about and Mr. Hoxie, at the earnest solicitation of Mr. Wm. E. Dodge and others, took charge of the International Railroad then building in Texas. He remained with this road some twelve years. By his economical management and wise forethought he succeeded in making this road one of the best in Texas, greatly strengthening himself in the estimation of both the stock and bondholders. The International was at this time of no small importance, embracing in its system seven hundred and eighty-two miles.

During this long connection, these twelve years, Mr. Hoxie endeared himself to the people of progressive ideas on account of his decided favor and approval of every enterprise for the development of the country and the advancement of the people. The Christian minister, the temperance lecturer, and the school-master were the recipients of his favors and his substantial support. "Put me down in favor of public schools and against whisky," was his pronounced position.

When the great Southwestern system was formed out of the International, the Texas Pacific, the Missouri Pacific, the St. Louis, Iron Mountain, Great Southern, and other roads, aggregating some six thousand five hundred miles, Mr. Gould selected Mr. Hoxie as one of the higher officials. His successful management continuing through years, his promotion keeping apace all the time, till at his death we find him Vice-President and General Manager, the sole executive of the entire system. While his death was doubtless occasioned by the arduous labor growing out of the intricate, the delicate problems of the great strike, 1886, on the system, the seeds of disease were sown long before this. His physical frame was never strong enough to fully meet the demands of his brain-power.

His greatest service to his

COMPANY, THE RAILROADS, AND THE COUNTRY

was performed in his exercise of a clear conception of right, and an inflexible adherence to this conception, his fairness and uniform courtesy to those opposing him. He was not unwilling to change, even to yield; his was not a stubborn, stolid obstinacy, it was a consistent firmness, based upon that highest of intellectual powers, an unerring perception of the truth, however surrounded and complicated with the environments of policy. These mental convictions were sustained by a necessary, an equal moral courage. In short, the life of Mr. Hoxie can be summed up in these three words—*firmness, fairness, faithfulness.*

The strike on the Southwestern system settled two great questions:

First, the right of employers, the owners of property, whether corporate or individual, to manage it in their own way under the laws.

Second, it settled also as divine a right as sacred a duty, that of employes to demand for their labor the greatest compensation ; this not granted, to stop work or continue as preferred.

In this contest there was a strange inconsistency upon the part of the employes, a discrimination in their own actions: If it were right to derail, to stop freight trains, why not right to stop, to destroy passenger and mail trains too?

Harmony restored, Mr. Hoxie sought to regain his shattered health by travel and by the aid of the best surgical skill in our country, but without restoration. Still, in his sick-chamber his mind went back to the faithful in his employment. One of his last inquiries, perhaps the very last, away in New York City, he telegraphed his Chief Superintendent in that department: "What has become of the boy-operator, E. H. Sladek, that saved bridge Thirty-seven on the night of the 14th of February, 1885?" The answer was sent: "He is occupying an humble position as night operator." Mr. Hoxie directed his promotion at once, he was sent to Sedalia, and occupies a lucrative position in the Superintendent's office. What a contrast! Napoleon on the lonely island of his last banishment, that stormy night on which his spirit left his doubly exiled body, kept muttering: "TÊTE DE L'ARMÉE," *Head of the Army.* Mr. Hoxie, forgetful of himself, inquires: What has become of the boy that saved the burning bridge?

But let those speak who were nearer, more competent to judge, and abler to express the appreciation of his associates and their estimate of him :

"*Whereas,* we have to day received the sad news of the death of H. M. Hoxie, first Vice-President of the Company ;

"*Whereas,* we have been associated with Mr. Hoxie as employes during the past five years, in which he has been connected with the management of the Missouri Pacific system as General Manager, third Vice-President, and first Vice-President, some of us having held positions in connection with his management of railways for a still longer period, and

"*Whereas,* the successful results which have attended his management of railway affairs are a source of gratification and pride to all who have worked in harmonious relations with him in carrying out the policy which he adopted, and

"*Whereas,* the uniform courtesy and kindness of Mr. Hoxie toward all employes with whom he came into personal relations, and the interest and appreciation shown by him in the work and welfare of all, whether personally known to him or not, have established between himself and those connected with his management the relationship of friends as well as co-laborers, therefore,

"*Resolved*, That in the death of H. M. Hoxie, first Vice-President, this Company has lost an executive whose ability, judgment, and strength of purpose have been of great and lasting benefit not only to this system of railways but to the railway interest of the entire country. The employes have lost a leader whose methods have tended to enlarge the dignity of the business in which we are engaged, and whose example has been an incentive to the attainment of the highest rewards of our profession through diligence, fidelity, and labor. We have lost a friend whose personal qualities endeared him to all who were brought into relations with him, and bound all who were within the circle of his official authority by ties of admiration and respect.

"*Resolved*, That the signatures of all who are present be attached to these resolutions, and that the original be forwarded to Mrs. Hoxie as a memorial."

These resolutions were signed by the officers and employes of the Missouri Pacific system.

GEORGE NOBLE

Was born in Franklin County, Pennsylvania, 1830. While yet a boy he embarked in the railroad business, commencing like all beginners at the bottom round of the ladder in a subordinate position on the Pennsylvania Railroad. He remained with this road until 1862 or 1863, when he severed his connection with it and went West to look after the mining interests of his uncle, Col. Thomas A. Scott, in California and Arizona. He returned from the West in 1866, and was appointed Superintendent of the eastern division of the Kansas Pacific Railroad. He served in this capacity until March 1, 1874, when he resigned to accept the general superintendency of the Texas & Pacific Railroad, which office he held until May, 1881. Col. Thos. A. Scott (1872) came into the possession of the Texas & Pacific Railroad, formed out of three distinct corporations, all together controlling only forty-four miles of road-bed. Thirteen miles were added before Col. Noble took charge (1874). Under his administration the line had reached, May, 1880, four hundred and forty-four miles; May, 1881, eight hundred miles with contracts perfected for the completion of the lines from New Orleans to El Paso; or in the aggregate, in January, 1882, arrangements had been made for the completion of the whole, one thousand four hundred and eighty-seven miles, virtually (via Southern Pacific) connecting the waters of the two oceans.

Col. Scott's health failing rapidly, he sold his interest in the Texas & Pacific to Mr. Gould.

With "the great projector" of the system gone, Col. Noble tendered his resignation, retired with his uncle. His connection with the road began at a most inauspicious time. It was virtually without road-bed, without rolling stock, and paralyzed with an accumulated debt, without credit, and without friends.

At the close of the seventh year he left it the longest line in the State.

Details are out of place here, but when it is estimated that it requires of material, twelve thousand cars, equal to one hundred and twenty thousand tons for each one hundred miles, equivalent to twelve million tons hauled one mile, some conception of the extra work done by the road can be gained, and all in addition to a heavy commercial traffic besides. All this extra transportation had to be provided for by the General Superintendent through his subordinates.

What a grand peace army!

Still all were not sunshiny days. Col. Noble had in that great army discordant, discontented men. When the strike of 1877 swept over the whole country, the Texas & Pacific, with other roads in the State, suffered its full share of loss of property and traffic.

An incident occurring then must not be omitted. Col. Noble was absent, returning on Saturday night. Sunday morning he was met by a committee of the men making certain demands. His reply, so characteristic of him, was: "No, gentlemen, I will not give you an answer on the Sabbath day. I do not engage to transact any business on that day, but if you will wait until to-morrow morning (Monday) I will give you a reply." The excited crowd withdrew. He went to church as usual. Monday he gave his answer, and men, who the previous day were frenzied with their imaginary wrongs, throwing their hats into the air, hurrahed for George Noble.

It was a fixed habit of the Colonel never to go to his office on Sunday, never to transact any business on this day. In the morning he attended Sabbath-school, and at 11 o'clock he was in his accustomed seat listening to his pastor as he dispensed the light and truth of the Gospel.

For nearly five years after his resignation he engaged in private business, having large interests in both mining and cattle.

The Texas & Pacific going into the hands of receivers, January, 1886, Governor John C. Brown called again to his aid his tried friend, believing that the *builder* was the best *rebuilder*, and hence we find the Colonel put as agent of the receivers, and soon as General Manager of the Texas & Pacific, with headquarters at Dallas. The work of rebuilding had hardly begun before upon them was the "the strike," which, although originating upon the Texas & Pacific, was soon transferred to the Missouri Pacific, or Southwestern system. The Texas & Pacific, being in the hands of the United States Court, received the prompt and efficient protection of the Government, and the interference was of short duration.

Still, while the whole people were excited over the troubles, railroad managers and employes alike, Col. Noble stood in the storm with all his senses about him, firm, unembarrassed—looked upon as a reliable friend by the employes, and known to be faithful by the employers. His address, his work, his uniform good temper did much toward bringing about harmony. Like Neptune of the seas, his very presence calmed the tumultuous crowd, and dispelled the angry passions of the excited multitude.

His loss to the people among whom he lived, and for whom he worked, can not be estimated, and there will not be an employe on the railroad of which he was one of the heads, who will not feel that a friend truly is gone.

Visiting his office a few days since, the draped walls, the vacant chair, all, all too truthfully forced upon me the realization, and involuntarily I repeated :

> " But, O, for the touch of a vanished hand
> And the sound of a voice that is still ! "

But let the man of God, one of his spiritual advisers, add his tribute :

" It was my privilege to have known our deceased brother for many years. To know him was to love him. His friendship honored those who were allowed to share it. He was a brave defender of good government, yet always with respectful regard for the rights of others. To his superiors in office he was loyal and true, to his equals generous and courteous, to his subordinates considerate and kind. While a master of minute detail in matters of business, he grasped with the mind of a statesman measures of wide policy. He was the friend of Texas. He loved her climate ; he loved her soil. He was among the first to perceive her grand possibilities and to execute measures by which their realization became practicable. His mind was early aware of her vast latent resources, and his best years were given to perfecting agencies for their development. But why speak of these things with my stammering tongue? The growing towns from Texarkana to El Paso, owing their prosperity largely to his genius, weave the chaplet of laurel we lay upon his brow. The happy families all along the line, helped to comfort by his toil, place their sprig of evergreen within his sepulcher. The laborers, who loved to serve beneath his gentle hand, gem with tears the floral honors on his bier. This is the homage which virtue alone can attain, and is rendered only to the good. He is not dead but sleepeth; not lost to us, but gone before. He filled out the rounded requirements of God's law. 'What doth the Lord require of thee but to do justly, and to love mercy, and to walk humbly with thy God?' No man ever accused him of an injustice to the value of a hair; none was ever weak who did not experience his mercy; no glance of pride ever burned in his eye. Such men are rare in any age. It is the glory of ours to have produced this one, and we lay him down to rest with the best homage of our grateful but afflicted hearts, a recognition of his worth.

"Rest in peace, and let eternal light shine upon thee, and the glory of the everlasting day gather round about thee: Thy example is our incentive to noble deeds, thy memory our benediction."

G. J. FOREACRE

Was born at Rainsborough, Ohio, February 19, 1828. Early in the "fifties" he removed from Ohio to Atlanta, Georgia, beginning work with the stage line between that city and Montgomery, Alabama. He remained with the stage line a short time only, and then accepted a position as section boss on the Central Railroad. This he filled with credit to himself, and with such satisfaction to the company that in a short time he was appointed conductor.

The appointment was quickly followed by an order from the manager promoting him to the Atlanta agency.

While serving in this capacity he manifested that peculiar tact, a knowledge of men and business, the ability to manage, to direct, which made him sought by many roads. As agent of the road he was upon the eve of being again promoted when the war broke out. Although an Ohio man, he had lived long enough in Georgia to become thoroughly identified with her interests, and when the time for action came he enlisted and went to the front.

In 1861 he left Atlanta as Captain of company B of the famous Seventh Georgia regiment, and throughout the sanguinary contest was unwavering in his fidelity to the Southern cause. He was a gallant soldier, and was

4

wounded severely in the first battle of Manassas. His illness, consequent upon this wound, was painful and protracted, and at times his life was despaired of by his friends. When but partially restored to health he resumed his place in the army and was subsequently promoted to the colonelcy. The war ended, he wisely accepted the situation and went bravely to work to repair his broken fortunes.

Although Atlanta was in ashes he believed she would become a thriving, busy city, that she was not only the "Gate City," but the railroad center of the Southeast.

The wound received at Manassas was still annoying him to such an extent that his activity was greatly impaired. He purchased a farm near Atlanta and started the successful Sugar Creek Paper Mills.

Here, while his health was recovering, he declined several fine railroad positions, but after growing strong and sufficiently restored, as he thought, he accepted a place with the Central Railroad again, as General Agent.

During this time the Montgomery & West Point Railroad, then a long line of some two hundred miles with its branches, was in such a condition that it must be either repaired or abandoned. Mr. Charles T. Pollard, its president, applied to Mr. Wadley, of the Central, to let his company have Col. Foreacre for this important and expensive work, requiring the rarest combination of economic, executive, and administrative ability. Mr. Wadley consented, and Col. Foreacre from June, 1870, to April, 1872, addressed himself to this difficult task.

When he took charge, the fact that a train arrived on time was the agreeable surprise—not to come at all was the rule.

Col. Foreacre was a man of magnificent physique, of splendid personal appearance, of frank and easy address. He possessed a high practical knowlege of the work he was about to undertake. Once a poor employe, he had the liveliest interest in the employes, and soon became acquainted with every man on the road.

Before a train would leave the depot he would personally interview the engineer, examine the engine, see for himself that every thing was "all right," then with an approving smile he would say, "Jack, try to get over to-day."

The result was the train steamed out with every body in a good humor, and a determination to look out for and avoid running recklessly over the bad places. Within less than three years this road (now the Western Railroad of Alabama) was the best equipped and made the quickest time and surest connections of any in the State or in the South.

Here Col. Forcacre showed his economic management in lengthening the runs. He saw the same cars over the same gauge roads could be advantageously handled by the same train hands and with more comfort to the passengers. Hence the trip from Atlanta to Montgomery (heretofore two separate managements with two separate crews) could be run as one solid through train. This was done, and with such success that soon after leaving the "Western" he secured, by his personal influence, a through sleeping-car line from the North to the South, inaugurating the line from Washington to New Orleans via the Kenesaw route. This was really the pioneer line, using a car-hoist to overcome the broken gauge at Lynchburg, Virginia. It was also at his suggestion that the first sleeping-car line from Boston to Florida was established. And to this arrangement to-day Florida owes her popularity as a winter resort for invalids.

It was during his connection with the "Western" that his interest in schools and colleges became known to the writer. The Agricultural and Mechanical College of the State was to be located by the legislature, and, with four other towns and cities competing, Auburn was an applicant. His idea was that the college would be a source of revenue as well as an ornament to his road. Its location at Auburn has verified his anticipation. It is one of the most popular and flourishing institutions in the State. Educational gatherings all along his lines received his personal recognition and his strong support.

From the "Western" he returned to the "Central" and was Superintendent of the Atlanta Division. From April, 1875, to March, 1877, he was General Manager of the Washington City, Virginia Midland & Great Southern Railroad; while, returning to his home, from March, 1877, to April, 1881, he was General Manager of the Atlanta & Charlotte Air Line Road. During his connection with this road he projected many smaller lines, becoming Superintendent of the Georgia Pacific.

He entered the service of the Baltimore & Ohio Railroad, January 1, 1884, as the General Superintendent of the Trans-Ohio Division, with headquarters at Newark, Ohio. This position he held till his death.

The Virginia Midland was really a Baltimore & Ohio line, and his return to this company was a reciprocal gratification.

Here, besides having a larger sphere, he had a company that was stable in its management, progressive enough, conservative enough, appreciating and rewarding diligent and faithful officials.

Col. Foreacre possessed those great prime requisites of all successful managers. He was a man of marked intellectual vigor, conscientious in the discharge of every duty, inflexible in his adherence to the right, unswerving in his support of order and good government. He had a heart of womanly tenderness, dispensing on all occasions with an open hand to the calls of deserving charity. With a most happy temper and pleasant deportment he won his way without effort into the respect and love of every one whom he met.

He loved Atlanta. It was the home of his adoption. The field of his greatest efforts and most successful triumphs. The graves of his children were there, and naturally he desired that his last resting place should be there. Loving and devoted friends saw that his wish should be carried out. His was one of the largest, if not the very largest funeral procession ever witnessed in that city. Citizens of high and low degree, senators, governors, all were present to show their appreciation of the life and their profound sorrow at the death of G. J. Foreacre.

Fit inscription for his tomb would be :

"Mark the perfect man and behold the upright; for the end of that man is peace."

CONCLUSION.

H. M. Hoxie, George Noble, G. J. Foreacre were alike poor boys, industrious youths, good citizens, Christian gentlemen (consistent members respectively of the Episcopal, Presbyterian and Methodist Church). They alike so directed circumstances as to become honored, because most useful to their country in their day and generation.

Young man, in their lives you have the key of your own success!

"From Hell Gate to Gold Gate
And the Sabbath unbroken,
A sweep continental
And the Saxon yet spoken."

Whether on the *trail* of "'49," or on the *rail* of "'69," or by the tedious *voyage* around "the Horn," our mother tongue has had much to do in the occupation of this continent.

There left Boston, Friday (4:30 P. M.), July 6, 1888, under Mr. Charles A. Brown, of the Chicago, Milwaukee & St. Paul Railway, as manager for the New England States, a train consisting of eight Pullmans and a baggage car for San Francisco. This train did not travel as fast as the one (centennial year) making the time between New York and San Francisco, 3,317 miles, in 83 hours and 23 minutes, three days and a half (3.47) or forty miles an hour, but, stopping at many points of interest, spending whole days in cities, reached San Francisco Tuesday, July 16th (4:30 P. M.), with 231 passengers, all delighted with the safety, comfort, and pleasure of the trip.

(53)

There were trains from the Lakes, trains from the Gulf, trains from the Prairies, trains from all points of the educational compass, until there were gathered and housed *within* the Golden Gate *twenty thousand* souls.

Not all of these were teachers — they were all learners, however, and carried home with them lessons of wisdom more precious than the gold of Ophir, more enduring than the riches of "the silver satrap of the Sierras."

One agency, a great factor in the success of this meeting, was the Palace Car. Travel by night as well as by day, economy of time, made the sleeping car a necessity, and the inventive genius of man was not long in solving the question.

Without entering into a discussion — leaving out all controversy — it seems that Mr. Woodruff was the first to conceive and to carry out practically his idea of a sleeping car. It is not denied that both Mr. Wagner and Mr. Pullman profited by Mr. Woodruff's invention; and while, doubtless, the very first attempt to furnish the railway traveller a place to sleep was upon the Cumberland Valley Railroad of Pennsylvania, Mr. George M. Pullman early comprehended the real magnitude of the problem, and set about its solution.

In 1864 he perfected plans for what was to be a radical change even in sleeping cars. He built at a cost then thought to be a fabulous sum for the purpose, $18,000, the "Pioneer."

This car being wider and higher than any heretofore in use, required changes on the part of the railroads in their bridges and culverts. This was cheerfully done by the roads; the travelling public now demanded this sleeper.

In 1867 the Pullman Car Company was organized. About the same time the Wagner Company came into the field, furnishing sleepers for the Vanderbilt and connecting lines.

Sleepers by night, luxurious couches, suggested spacious drawing-rooms for day travel, and the Parlor Car is furnished. And now Hotel Cars are needed, and the Pullman Company introduced the first, aptly named the "President." This car was put into service on the Great Western Railway of Canada, 1867.

The Hotel Car was rather cramped. The tables, portable, had to be arranged between the seats; hence the Dining Car "Delmonico" makes its appearance, 1868.

But to reach this car, passengers — men, women, and children—had to pass through other cars, cross over platforms with more or less inconvenience and positive danger. And now another demand. Not only a "covered way," but "*guards*" must be furnished, and a *tunnelled* train—"vestibuled" called — is the latest product of Mr. Pullman's fruitful evolutions.

The first road running these was the Pennsylvania (1886).

On these trains carrying sleeping cars, a dining car fitted out with a smoking saloon, a library with books, desks, and writing material, a bathroom and a barber shop, an American citizen travels in as princely style as does the crowned head in Europe on his "royal special train," and at figures that should always be pasted in the hats of party politicians, chronic disturbers of the peace and quiet of our people.

COMPARATIVE RAILROAD AND PALACE CAR RATES.

COUNTRIES.	First Class.	Second Class.	Third Class.	ROUTES.	Distance in Miles.	Berth Fare.
	Cents.	Cents.	Cents.			
United Kingdom	4.42	3.20	1.94	Paris to Rome...............	901	$12 75
France	3.86	2.88	2.08	New York to Chicago....	912	5 00
Germany.............	3.10	2.32	1.51	Calais to Brindisi..........	1,374	22 25
United States......	2.18	*		Boston to St. Louis.........	1,330	6 50

* The first-class passengers constitute about 99 per cent of the travel in this country.

The policy inaugurated under the following action doubtless had much to do in the increased and increasing success of the association :

"Under the head of resolutions, the following was offered by Professor Alexander Hogg, of Texas, and unanimously adopted:

"In order to effect a better and more uniform system of special rates upon the various railroads and other methods of conveyance, to secure, so far as possible, some definite concert of action upon the part of the authorities of the various lines of trans-portation for the next annual meeting of the association, therefore, be it

"*Resolved*, By this association, that a committee of seven be appointed by the president, to be known and styled as "The Department of Transportation."

"*Resolved*, That one of them by appointment shall be the president of the depart-ment, and that the remaining six shall act as chairmen of the six districts to be here-after determined, and they shall have power to appoint an assistant or assistants to aid them in properly organizing and perfecting this department.

"The author in presenting the resolutions said : That heretofore there had been no proper understanding upon this subject of transportation, which was one of the most important as well as the most vital business points of the association, and that this failure grew out of the neglect on the part of the association to properly present the claims of the members, coming as they do from all parts and quarters of the United States, to what is known as special or excursion rates; that it was true at first sight there seemed to be insurmountable difficulties in the way, but that it was not so at all; that the great carrying community was deeply interested in this educational work, and that if properly acquainted with its objects, that a system could be per-fected; that instead of hundreds of teachers there would be thousands in attendance on these gatherings; that the liberality of these corporations was greatly misunder-stood; that as a general rule — if there was merit, if there was any good reason why they should grant special rates — they had never failed to do it. He hoped that the plan proposed would meet with the cordial indorsement of the association; and that the great carrying interests of our country would be invited to show their appre-ciation of and their interest in the education of the common country as represented by this, The National Educational Association."—*Proceedings of National Educational Association, Louisville,* 1877.

The "insurmountable difficulties in the way" were studied just like any other problem, and while the very best arrangements were not secured "for the next annual meeting," nor at the next, still the transportation has been the main question in selecting the place of meeting, till now, through the com-binations—traffic associations—not only is *one fare* granted for the round trip, with side excursions, some for less than a fare, but the railroads have become the financial agents, the collectors of the association (all tickets having a *coupon* for the "plus two dollars" membership fee).

This arrangement made the Madison meeting the first great meeting, reaching the "thousands," and San Francisco the greatest up to date.

The railroads have shown their interest in the education of our common country in this, the finest and largest collection of "systems" and "methods," in bringing together the leading and controlling spirits of the three hundred thousand men and women engaged in the responsible training of the twenty millions of children for the highest duties known to the American citizen, the casting of an intelligent ballot.

Again, as late as 1850 there was not a mile of railroad west of the Mississippi. The "centennial year" train could not have made the trip "3.47 days" before 1869—neither could the great National Association have collected its teachers—nor could the thousands, millions, who now traverse the continent without comprehending the time and the distance, have done so, but for the undertakings—the accomplishments of the projectors and builders of the Pacific Railways. Commercial interests had time and again suggested these great enterprises, and men *then* called "visionary" for the lack of the later coinage, "crank," had sent out reconnoitering parties—who made preliminary surveys; but the necessity for so stupendous a work was not brought home to the nation until the Southern States attempted to *secede*—to divide this Union by a geographical, an imaginary line east and west. This action forced the Government to lend its aid in constructing a real line—*two lines* of steel rail from the Missouri to the Pacific—thus uniting by Art what long since had been decreed by Nature—the perpetuity of this Republic.

A faithful description of the work is beyond the scope and purpose of this humble contribution.

To determine the location alone of a route for the Union Pacific, 15,000 miles of instrumental and preliminary lines were run; 25,000 miles of reconnoisances were travelled. The engineers of the Central Pacific had to do the same thing, and in the face of the same difficulties, both parties in sight of the native tribes, less hospitable than the deserts and mountains.

But the preliminaries completed, the work of construction begins, and for five years, under the leadership of Gen. G. M. Dodge and Charles Crocker respectively, armies of men, roll-calls of thousands, Teuton, Celt, and Celestial (the latter the most willing worker), with shovels and pick-axes, the implements of peace and progress, are marching west and east over boundless plains, through waterless deserts, and up the rugged mountain with its whelming snow-drifts.

But these *giants*, instead of piling Pelion upon Ossa so as to scale Olympus, by a system of *loops* and *tunnels* made step-ladders of the lesser peaks, not to ascend to heaven, but to place *among* the heavens a smooth path, "a plain way" for all tongues and all nations, and that, too, for all coming centuries.

A loop is a happy device of engineering to go *through* a mountain by going *around* it—a tunnel, to go *over* a mountain by going *through* it.

"The end draweth nigh," and victory complete over nature's barriers is proclaimed upon the morning of the 9th of May, 1869, when near the head of the great Salt Lake they lay down the last tie of polished laurel bound with silver bands. Nevada sends a silver spike, California sends two of gold, while Arizona, more practical than either, sends three—one of silver, one of gold, and one of iron.

"The silver sledge gleams in the air, and the blow that follows is heard farther than any other blow ever struck by mortal man, and all over the continent the ringing of bells and booming of cannon simultaneously announce the tidings of the feat."* Instinctively the locomotives salute each other, touch pilots, and with a hearty hurrah—a shrill whistle—add their congratulations upon the consummation of this union, this wedlock of the oceans.

---

* The last spike and the hammer that drives it are in electric communication with nearly all the fire alarms in the country.

The costs of these two enterprises respectively, the Union Pacific about $39,000,000, and the Central Pacific about $140,000,000, but in the two years, 1872 and 1873, there were saved to the Government alone in the transportation of postal and war materials, $3,789,788, or over twenty per cent upon first cost.

The builders of this highway, elated by continued success, flushed with recent victory, soon again are found approaching each other from "the West" and "the East," and the Southern Pacific and the Texas Pacific, under respectively the same leaders, with the same associates, meet a second time, 1882, at SIERRA BLANCA, and another transcontinental railway is furnished "on or near the 32° parallel of latitude."

Upon the Southern Pacific the engineering and building, too, if possible, were even more difficult than upon either the Union or Central Pacific. The cut of the Te-hachapi Love Knot is here inserted for those teachers who are still in the *Kindergarten*. It is a fine *object* lesson. A description as given by a great teacher is added:

TEHACHAPI PASS LOVE KNOT.

"Now we look down upon four tracks we have come, and now we look up upon three tracks we are going, that are forever crossing themselves like a confused witness." ... "The double-stranded thread on which these heights are strung, called the Loop, is three thousand seven hundred and ninety-five feet long, a great double-bow knot of steel."

NEW ROADS.—In our country railroad building (1888) has not kept pace with previous years; not so much as in 1887, but is even more active in foreign countries.

It is announced that "The Tientsin Railway, the first practical railway in China, which was formally opened in October, 1888, is eighty-one miles long. This road extends from Tientsin to Tonsham."

It is but fair to believe that this railway work is the dawn of a new civilization within the heretofore closed walls of this mighty empire. The *returning* Celestial may have had something to do with it.

South America perhaps, in Peru and Bolivia, is prosecuting the most stupendous railway enterprises of this era.

It is gratifying to note that the suggestion found on page 19 of this address is now fulfilling; roads are building, up into Alaska, and from the west through Siberia, the object is said to be a connection by steamer crossing Behring's Strait, shortening the passage to the East by traveling west.

RAILROADING ABOVE THE ARCTIC CIRCLE.—"An important engineering enterprise, now in progress, is a railroad to the Arctic Circle. The Swedish and Norwegian railroad now building from Lulea, on the Gulf of Bothnia, to Lufloden, on the North Sea, is partly situated within the Arctic Circle, and is some 1,200 miles farther north than any railroad in Canada."

Since the railroad is the only invading army that never breaks its line of communication, never "changes its base," why not attempt, not to reach the North Pole, but the "open polar sea," by building a railway to it. Such "an expedition" not able to go forward, could at least retreat.

SAFETY APPLIANCES.—Great progress has been made in the past two years in safety appliances. The deadly coal stove has been superseded—not on all trains, but a beginning; a successful test has been made of steam heating. The first road to adopt steam heat was the Elevated, in New York; the next, the Boston & Albany.

An official of the latter gives the following: "We equipped two trains in the fall of 1886, and ran them through that winter. In the spring of 1887 the contract was made with the Martin Steam Heating Company to equip all our trains as fast as possible. In the fall of 1887 our New York train was equipped with steam heat, and now most of our passenger trains are so equipped."

The same official adds: "The electric light for trains was first tried by the Pennsylvania Railroad in 1884 on a few drawing-room cars only. The first entire train to be lighted by electricity in America (and as far as known in the world) ran from Boston to New York, over the Boston & Albany (Springfield Line), March 30, 1887. This train has been running continuously since."

This light bids fair to become universal.

In this advance heat and light have travelled together, the result of their merciful mission, has been greater security to the life and comfort of the passengers. Meantime, the safety of the exposed and too-long-neglected train hand has received the consideration due him, and the following is quoted in evidence that legislatures are looking into this matter: "The bill compelling all roads operating in the State of New York to equip their freight cars with automatic couplers has become a law. Until November 1, 1890, is given the roads to comply with the provisions of the law. The penalty for non-compliance is $500 for each offense."

When we consider the great army of brakemen exposed to heat and cold, to sunshine and storm (on the cars, *between* the cars, UNDER the cars), and the number of these faithful fellows daily maimed or killed outright, the universal adoption of the automatic coupler must be hailed as the most *advanced* advance in railway safety appliances.

SUNDAY TRAINS.—This is perhaps the most difficult problem, being both a religious and an economic question at the same time, that the managers of the roads have to confront. It is not true that the managers are responsible for Sunday trains. They would prefer no sound of whistle or engine-bell be heard on their lines on the Sabbath. It is true that the patrons, the travellers, the shippers, are responsible. Says a late writer:

"Competition is perhaps more severe between railroad companies than between any other class of business or carriers in the world. The merchant in Chicago, who desires to ship to Liverpool one hundred car loads of grain, knowing that his steamer sails from Boston on a certain day, and the choice of route rests between two roads, one of which runs trains on Sunday and the other does not, would not hesitate long in giving the business to the road running the Sunday trains. The Detroit merchant, going to his store this morning, finding some article of merchandise called for by his customers which he can not obtain in the city, telegraphs to New York or Boston, for example, therefor. It is shipped by what road? By the road bringing it in the least time for the least money. Of two roads, one running Sunday trains and the other not, which will probably get the business?"

Again: In California you receive a dispatch calling you to the bedside of some dear one in Boston, or any city east of the Mississippi, would you purchase a ticket by the road that lays over on Sunday in Ogden or Omaha?

Efforts are now making on several of the trunk lines to withdraw as many trains as possible from their roads on Sunday. This can be done in many cases without detriment to shippers, and will be done in all cases when all merchants will openly say: " We will not patronize nor have any thing to do with the railroad that runs Sunday trains." This change must come through public opinion—through press and pulpit. The transcontinental trains between the Atlantic and the Pacific in the prompt delivery of the mails —in the interests of the public—ought, perhaps, to run; and within the States trains laden with perishable freight, or suffering live stock, should be allowed to reach destination without detention, with all dispatch.

Whatever may be the solution to this problem fraught with so many difficulties, surrounded by so many conflicting interests, it is safe to say that the railroad managers will cheerfully do their part in bringing about a speedy and a just settlement of the question.

GIFTS TO SCHOOLS.—Mr. W. H. Vanderbilt left in his will, additional to his former gifts, $200,000 to be added to the general endowment of the Vanderbilt University. Cornelius, the grandson, desiring to fit the University to educate the whole man, liberal provisions having already been made for the departments of Letters and Theology, gave (1888) $20,000 for building and equipping "Mechanical Hall," the second building of the Engineering Department, and $10,000 for additions to the University library. Thus father, son, and grandson have contributed, and to this one institution, $1,480,000.

THE DEATH OF MR. CHARLES CROCKER.—The National Educational Association, the success of which was so largely due to the management of the Southern Pacific Railway, had just adjourned. Many of the members were still enjoying the hospitalities of new-made friends on the coast, or at the numerous pleasure resorts in the mountains, when it was announced that "at the Hotel del Monte, Mr. Charles Crocker died, 14th August, 1888, aged 65 years and 11 months."

The resolutions passed by the Board of Directors of the Southern Pacific Company, of which he was Second Vice-President, set forth:

First: The irreparable loss the company has sustained.

Second: The great work accomplished by him as director in the construction of thousands of miles of railroads, thereby rendering millions of acres of land valuable.

Third: His personal characteristics, determination, directness, frankness, fairness; that the most exacting integrity and strictest honesty were interwoven in every muscle and fiber of his being; that his uprightness of character and sincerity of purpose commanded the admiration and respect of those who knew him best, and were a constant inspiration to the officers and employés who were subject to his direction.

Fourth: That for his abilities and achievements they have the highest respect and admiration; for his high character and broad humanity they hold his memory in great affection, and that even in this day of sorrow they are truly thankful that they have enjoyed the benefit of his personal friendship and experience in all their official relations.

His charities, as gathered from press and persons near him:

Some eleven years ago Mr. Crocker purchased The Ward Natural History and Geological Collection for $50,000, presenting the same to The California Academy of Science. To the same institution he gave $20,000 as a fund, the interest of which should be spent in giving employment to such persons as in their devotion to scientific pursuits have become incapacitated for active life.

This fund is known as "The Crocker Scientific Investigation Fund." In 1885 he presented to the Boys' and Girls' Aid Society $33,000 as a fund, independent of an annual sum, for its support. The same year he rebuilt the dome of the Golden Gate Park, destroyed by fire, 1882. The specific amount contributed to this could not be ascertained, Mr. Crocker under his own personal supervision furnishing the material, the architect, and workmen.

His private beneficence was even greater. In addition to a large list of old friends, to whom he gave regularly, he furnished his wife, monthly, $5,000, to be distributed by her in charities of her own selection. It was his custom to send checks every Christmas to all the Homes and Orphan Asylums, the only condition enjoined was that no publicity should be given as to the donor. When, in October, 1885, the establishment of H. S. Crocker & Co., stationers, was totally destroyed, in which, while the largest sufferer, he did not stop to inquire the extent of his loss, but telegraphed from New York $5,000 as a gift to the families of the two brave firemen who had perished at the fire.

While always affable and pleasant, Mr. Crocker sometimes became facetious, and in the goodness of his heart often gave when he doubted the propriety of the act. It is related by one present, that on one occasion two ladies seeking an audience with him were detained in the waiting-room, and on its becoming known to him, he said: "Show them in immediately; it does not do to keep ladies waiting." They had come in the interest of the "Old Ladies' Home." Mr. Crocker smilingly asked how much he was to give. "Oh, any thing you please; we will be perfectly content with any sum." Whereupon he responded: "Another cool robbery," and, drawing his check-book, he wrote and handed them an order for $2,500.

In 1887, when it became known that the Sacramento Orphan Asylum needed money, he sent his check of $1,000; and the very last act of his business life was to sign a check of $250 for the Free Kindergarten School of Sacramento.

A very fitting close of his benevolent career. Sacramento was the home of his early activities: it was here that the four life-long associates, Huntington, Hopkins, Stanford, and Crocker projected and matured the plans for constructing, and from which as a basis of supplies was built, the Central Pacific Railway.

As if preparing the State for a happier race and greater destiny, he and his associates levelled or tunnelled mountain chains, penetrated the forests, turned the channels of rivers, checked the ocean's inroads, changed the whole face of this Western Empire, until now is fully realized the poet's dream:

> " Beneath the rocky peak that hides
>   In clouds its snow-flecked crest,
> Within these crimson crags abides
>   An Orient in the West."

www.ingramcontent.com/pod-product-compliance
Lightning Source LLC
Chambersburg PA
CBHW021525090426
42739CB00007B/785